From Christendom to Apostolic Mission

Pastoral Strategies for an Apostolic Age

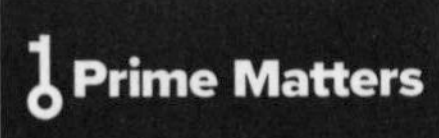

First published in 2020

Published in the United States of America
by University of Mary Press
7500 University Drive
Bismarck, ND 58504
www.umary.edu

ISBN: 978-0-9988728-9-6

Nihil Obstat & Imprimatur

+ The Most Reverend David D. Kagan, D.D., P.A., J.C.L
Bishop of Bismarck
28 January 2020

The *Nihil Obstat* and *Imprimatur* are official declarations that a book or pamphlet is free of doctrinal or moral error. No implication is contained therein that those who granted them agree with the content or statements expressed.

Design: Jerry Anderson

Printed in Canada

Cover Image

THE FIRST CHRISTIANS IN KIEV

by Vasily Perov, 1880
Oil on canvas, 156 x 243 cm
The Russian Museum, St. Petersburg, Russia

Preface

Brothers and sisters, Christendom no longer exists!

— POPE FRANCIS (to the Roman Curia)

I WRITE these words from the silence and seclusion of a 30-day retreat in the city of Jerusalem. From the window of my room I can see the sun rising over Mount Zion and the Benedictine Abbey of the Dormition of Mary.

There are on Zion places I cannot see from here. In the bright morning shadow of the Abbey, tucked just behind it, is the chamber believed to hold the Tomb of King David, the Lord's beloved. And up an adjacent staircase is the Cenacle, the upper room marking the site of the Last Supper and Pentecost, the birthplace of the Eucharist and the Church.

It was around the Cenacle that the very first generation of Christians gathered, and they are said to have returned to and settled in that neighborhood after the destruction of Jerusalem in A.D. 70, when the remains of the Holy City were little more than a campground for the Roman Tenth Legion.

I think of them, those brave men and women of faith, so in love with the Risen Lord, from whom the Gospel went out to all the earth. They were living in a heap of ashes, the great Temple reduced to piles of enormous stone, the whole world hostile to their belief and way of life. But they burned brightly with hope, for they had the Holy Spirit.

In the midst of these days of retreat, my mind vivid with such memories, I have taken up to read once again a manuscript that I now entrust to you. It is the fruit of long discussion among a group of good friends who love Christ and the Church, who have pondered together the circumstances in which believers in Jesus now find ourselves.

In 1974, Archbishop Fulton Sheen said in a conference, "We are at the end of Christendom. Not of Christianity, not of the Church, but of Christendom. Now what is meant by Christendom? Christendom is economic, political, social life as inspired by Christian principles. That is ending — we've seen it die." But he went on to say, "These are great and wonderful days in which to be alive. … It is not a gloomy picture — it is a picture of the Church in the midst of increasing opposition from the world. And therefore live your lives in the full consciousness of this hour of testing, and rally close to the heart of Christ."

This hour of testing calls us to recover for our age the apostolic mindset and the bright hope of those first Christians of the Cenacle. The thoughts and principles in this essay are meant as a fraternal encouragement and help to all those engaged in such work. I can only say, with gratitude, that insofar as this vision has guided our work with students at the University of Mary, we have seen tremendous fruit.

Praised be Jesus Christ!

Monsignor James Shea, President
The University of Mary

From Jerusalem, 11 July 2019
The Feast of Saint Benedict,
Father of Monasticism in the West,
Patron of Christian Europe

Table of Contents

Introduction

Ours is not an age of change, but a change of the ages.

— THE APARECIDA DOCUMENT
The Bishops of Latin America and the Caribbean

THE CHURCH, from the time of its founding by Christ, has been ever surrounded by conflict and engaged in struggle. At every point, the One who came as light into darkness to establish a kingdom of truth and love has been opposed by the darkness. The light continues to shine; its origin is in God himself, and the darkness cannot overcome it (cf. Jn 1). But the extent of that light, the way it sheds its rays, the kind of opposition it encounters and therefore the means it uses to keep its light shining and shed its influence abroad, changes from place to place and age to age. It is therefore important for those who are members of Christ's body, who share in his divine life and so are called by him to be the light of the world (cf. Mt 5), to take thought for the times in which they live and to devise pastoral and evangelistic strategies suited to those times.

This is a task for every generation; but when social arrangements and the Church's influence on the societies she inhabits are relatively stable, relations and strategies may hold good over a long period of time. In *an age of change*, the Church needs to pay attention to the modes by which she carries on her graced battle to be sure she is not 'fighting yesterday's war,' using strategies that for whatever reason are outmoded and have become ineffective. In a time that could be called *a change of the ages*, this duty becomes urgent. We are currently living in such a time. We are watching many long-standing arrangements and relations being altered, sometimes with surprising rapidity.

There has been a great deal of conversation in the Church about the "New Evangelization." Pope Paul VI first articulated the idea when he noted that Europe had once again become mission territory. It gained significant momentum under Pope John Paul II, who spoke of it often. Pope Benedict XVI established a Vatican dicastery for the New Evangelization, and the phrase has increasingly become a kind of catchword. The readiness with which the idea of a new evangelization has taken hold shows that there is a widespread sense of a need for a different strategy. Yet often enough the meaning of the term seems less than straightforward. Evangelization is clear enough, or ought to be: but what is meant by "new"?

Among other things:

We are dealing with the first culture in history that was once deeply Christian but that by a slow and thorough process has been consciously ridding itself of its Christian basis. Our society is full of many — including those baptized and raised with some exposure to faith — who believe that they have seen enough of Christianity to see that it has little to offer them. We are therefore not attempting to make converts from pagans; we are attempting to bring back to the Church those knowingly or unknowingly in the grasp of apostasy, a different and more difficult challenge. C. S. Lewis once described this difference as that between a man wooing a young maiden and a man winning a cynical divorcée back to her previous marriage. The situation is made yet more complex in that many who have abandoned Christianity and have embraced an entirely different understanding of the world still call themselves Christians.

Moreover, we are in the midst of a technological revolution that has radically altered the way people live and appears to hold in store yet more far-reaching effects on human life. This change goes much deeper than the obvious differences in the details of physical existence: automobiles instead of horses, electric light and central heating instead of hearth and candle, telephones and televisions and computers as regular features of life. The enormous change these and other technological developments have brought about in the daily organization of life has had its impact on all aspects of the human personality and on all social relationships, in ways that are probably too profound to entirely comprehend. Our view of ourselves, of the natural world, of our families, our work, our mental and emotional furniture, our hopes for this life, all have undergone a radical change. The elements and instruments of this change are well known. Developments in transportation, in information and communication technologies, in entertainment media, and in manufacturing have so changed our way of being that a person who lived a hundred years ago was closer both in modes of consciousness and in the daily rhythms of life to the time of Christ than to our own. Technological development has also brought about an attack, often unwittingly, on human nature itself. Long-standing assumptions about what it means to be human are under siege.

This extraordinary development in the applied sciences, especially in the area of electronic technology, has brought in its train an unprecedented explosion of images and information assailing each individual mind, even the youngest child's, laced with assumptions about how to be successful and what it means to live a good life. The denizen of the modern world is incessantly hounded and cajoled by gospels of various kinds, schemes of salvation and routes to happiness wrapped in highly attractive but often deceptive clothing.

It will be seen that the key battles our culture faces are intellectual ones. This fact can be hidden by the obvious moral character of some of them, but it is true nonetheless. Every age has been sorely tempted to sexual immorality; it has been left to our age to construct a sophisticated intellectual justification for sexual profligacy. All times have known the temptation to be cruel to children whose existence was inconvenient for the adults who cared for them; only our age has devised a way of thinking that has made the murder of children acceptable and even an act of moral goodness when enlisted in the campaign for personal autonomy. Every age has suffered from human pride and overreaching; only in our age have humans developed technologies and mindsets that are bent on recreating the human genetically and robotically from the ground up. These are intellectual wounds, and those who hope to make a Christian appeal to the members of modern societies need to mount an intellectual counterattack. "Intellectual" here does not primarily mean "academic." Our academic institutions are often so decayed in purpose (apart from technical training) that not much wisdom or light is to be hoped from them; for various reasons, they can tend to deform rather than enlighten the minds of those who come under their influence. Rather, what is needed is the sort of intellectual life that was characteristic of the Church in her early centuries, a life possessed to some degree by every Christian. It is not simply or primarily a matter of college degrees but of the conversion of the mind to a Christian vision of reality and of readiness to live out the ramifications of that vision. A compelling Christian narrative is called for, one that provides a counter to the secular vision, that helps Christians understand and fend off false gospels. There needs to be a re-articulation of the truth that can provide those who are languishing under the malnourishment of the modern spiritual diet a way out of their predicament.

It should be no surprise to us — in fact it should come to us as something expected — that the Church, which though possessing an ancient tradition and an unchanging faith is still the youngest and freshest institution on earth by virtue of the ever-new presence of the Holy Spirit within her, should respond to such a novel situation with new forms of life and missionary strategies to capture the contemporary age with her perennial truths. It is what the Church has always done, in the measure of the need of the day.

This essay is an attempt to contribute effective pastoral and evangelistic strategies to engage our time and our culture.

I

The Place of a Ruling Imaginative Vision in Human Cultures

EVERY HUMAN society possesses with more or less strength a moral and spiritual imaginative vision, a set of assumptions and a way of looking at things that is largely taken for granted rather than argued for. These fundamental assumptions provide the atmosphere the society's members breathe and the soil in which the various institutions of the society take root and grow. Such a vision is holistic, a way of seeing things. It is usually secured by a religion that orders the deepest questions, but it includes more than what we usually call religion: not only a moral code, but also an accepted ideal of the good person, clear categories of success and failure, economic and political values and practices, legal codes and public policy, manners and modes of entertainment. Such a vision is the property not just of a few specially educated people but of the whole society. Some will understand and be able to articulate it better than others, but all will possess it. In a vigorous civilization this imaginative vision is more or less a settled matter, and the longer it is settled, the more deeply and unconsciously it is assumed. When a culture's vision is seriously contested, the society will go into a crisis until its original vision is either reconstituted or overthrown and another overarching vision takes its place.

To call such a vision "imaginative" is not to say that it is "make-believe." It refers rather to the remarkable human capacity to maintain in our minds much that is not immediately in our surroundings. Animals are dominated by time and sense; their world is circumscribed by what is available to their senses at any given moment. But humans are capable of transcending the immediate circumstances of time and place and of carrying a whole world in their minds, reaching back into the past and going forward into the future, embracing other places and realizing even invisible realities. This is why each individual has been called a "microcosm" of the universe, because each of us carries a whole cosmos within us, and we gauge how we are to act depending on the features of that cosmos. Much of what it means to be converted in mind is to receive and embrace the Christian imaginative vision of the cosmos: to see the whole of the world according to the revelation given in Christ, and to act upon that sight with consistency.

It is typical that the majority of the members of a given society assume its imaginative vision without much difficulty, often unconsciously. A minority will be very zealous for the maintenance of the truths and practices embedded in the ruling vision, while a greater number will pay little conscious attention to them and will drift along with the prevailing current. But few will deny them outright.

To take a limited example: in the United States, democracy both as a governmental form and an ideal of life is part of our received vision. Most Americans can hardly imagine a different polity or way of looking at things: try suggesting that we would do best as a monarchy and see how far the suggestion goes or whether it can even be taken seriously. A relatively small number really understand what democracy means, what its possibilities and dangers are, or how to establish it and how to preserve it, but almost all assume it and order their lives under its influence. One might say something similar about our view of the importance of education, or of the priority of physical health, or of the ethical imperative to be concerned about the environment. Many don't pursue these ideals with much energy, yet they assume them. They don't posit a different vision even when they neglect them.

The ruling vision of a given society will have many sources: religion, philosophical currents, traditions that come down from long usage, social and political experience as it is distilled over time, as well as linguistic and geographic and artistic influences. What is important to note is that such a holistic vision, whether possessed by a society, or a group of people within a broader society, or an individual, is the basis of that society's or group's or person's *action.* The vision need not be — and often is not — fully consistent in its philosophical or religious principles; it may be that it cannot be easily distilled into a set of propositions or laid out as a coherent program for ordering a life or a society. What matters is that it gathers together an overall view such that the individual and the society are given a basis to move, to make decisions, to pursue one path rather than another. Its power is in its ability to hold together a world in a more or less compelling narrative. Those who are taking such action usually do not know why they find their way so obviously; they are under the influence of a set of first principles, often hidden away in their minds and acted *from* rather than discussed.

Another way of describing this is to note that each society, each group within a society, and each individual carries an inner narrative that provides a sense of meaning and direction. Because humans are creatures who make our way through space and time, who are by nature historical beings with a past and a future, we are necessarily involved in a kind of story, and we cannot escape the construction of a narrative that provides a compass and signposts along the way. There are no doubt better and worse narratives, and they are susceptible to examination and development over time; but none of us can function without a narrative of some sort, even if we might want to or claim to. For most, this personal narrative will be assumed, often unconsciously, from the broader society's ruling imaginative vision. As life goes on, depending on cast of mind and opportunities, some will bring various aspects of this inherited vision under scrutiny and either lay hold of it more firmly and with greater understanding or perhaps adjust it and amend it, even at times entirely rejecting it in order to embrace a different vision and a different narrative. But for the majority the ruling vision is never examined, because it is not known to exist. It is not so much something that is seen as something *through which* everything else is seen. It appears, if at all, as simply self-evident.

To point out the existence of such a largely unconscious ruling vision or narrative is not to complain about it: it has to be this way. Only the very few have the time and resources and talent to painstakingly sort out the foundations of a society's life or even the life of an individual. Yet everyone needs to act. This is one of the beneficial functions of traditions and cultural practices of all kinds, whether religious or national or familial. They bring forward for new members a tested vision of the whole of life and thereby give ready criteria for what is success and what is failure, for what needs to be considered in making decisions; in short, for action.

Pollsters often ask: Are things in general going in a good direction or a bad one? Is life in America, or on earth, getting better, getting worse, or staying about the same? The response to such a question always assumes a particular overall vision and a corresponding narrative, without which no possible answer could be given. The one who sees the main story of life as a battle for economic success and has sorted out plans that hinge upon ever-increasing possibilities of possessions and financial security will answer this question on the basis of economic variables: wealth is increasing and the possibilities for further increase look favorable into the future, so things are going well; stocks are down, markets are fragile, and inflation is high, so things are going badly. The one who sees the world as an arena in which the struggle for personal freedom is played out will evaluate the question on the basis of factors like the success or failure of democracy in America and around the world or the degree to which individual freedom is being ever better protected or ever more encroached upon. The one who sees the fundamental drama of life as an evolutionary process demanding the proper handling of the ecosystem in order to secure the further development of the human race will look to questions of pollution or climate change or sustainable use of resources. The one whose narrative involves a revelation of cosmic battle for souls between God and the devil will answer the question according to the advance or retreat of Christianity.

The same holds true at the individual level. Every time a person is asked the common question, "How are things? How is life going?" the answer is based upon some assumed narrative embedded in an overall vision of life, one that spells out what personal success and failure mean and how they are to be assessed.

An assumed narrative vision can be seen to be in play, whether in an individual or in a society as a whole, when a given proposition or way of acting is immediately either affirmed or ruled out of court without serious argument, even if it has not been self-evident to other individuals or to other human societies. To take a few current examples: slavery is a self-evident evil in America; we don't argue about it. If the suggestion were made that slavery was on the whole a good, or at least a neutral and necessary thing, it would not be met with careful argument; we would run it out the door, despite the fact that many human societies, including some now existing, have found justifications for it. On the other hand, we are now having to argue over ideas and practices whose worth (or lack of worth) would have seemed self-evident for many societies and in no need of argumentation, such as abortion or homosexual marriage. This is not to say that such questions are morally arbitrary, or that careful thought about them is unimportant, or that no arguments could or should be made for one view over another. It is rather to note that for the majority, arguments are not the main basis of action. When a given way of thinking or acting is part of an overall imaginative vision, it will be assumed as self-evident. Arguments, such as they are, will be marshaled to support the previously held vision, and challenges to it will tend either to be ignored or ridiculed and shouted down.

It has long been one of the primary aims of the western educational tradition to free the mind (hence the "liberal" arts, the arts that liberate) not from a ruling narrative, which is undesirable and impossible, but from unexamined assumptions that may make a ruling narrative irrational or incoherent. The collapse of such education in our time only means that we are frequently dealing with individuals and groups of people, often highly "educated," who are conspicuously unaware of their ruling visions and the assumptions they bring to questions of the day, and who are therefore little able to apply to those assumptions the kind of examination that could increase their clarity and purify them from irrationality. This clarifying role is one of the tasks of reason as regards faith. Faith gives us, from God himself, the overall narrative for the human race: who we are, who God is, what his purposes toward us are, how we have gotten into our current state, what God is doing about it, what is coming in the future, and therefore, how we should live. Reason keeps that narrative from wandering into superstition or bigotry or incoherency, such that it can provide a good and true basis for handling life.

Christendom and Apostolic Modes of Engagement

When the Christian narrative of the human drama and its corresponding moral order have become prominent in a given society and have come to provide, at least largely, that society's ruling vision, what emerges can be called a "Christendom culture." Some have used the term Christendom to refer to a society in which the Church is officially established in a confessional state — medieval England, say. Here is meant something broader. A Christendom society is one that goes forward under the imaginative vision and narrative provided by Christianity, whatever the specific polity concerning its establishment may be.

Christianity arose at a time when Israel, God's chosen people, was surrounded by a sophisticated Hellenistic culture with a strong ruling vision of its own, and during its first three centuries the Christian Church was to one degree or another in conflict with its surroundings. During this time the Church functioned in an apostolic mode, by which is meant that she was making her way against the current of the wider society and needed to articulate and maintain a distinct and contrasting vision. Those who were brought into the Church did more than embrace a set of moral principles or doctrinal statements. There was a need for a profound conversion of mind and imagination such that they saw *everything*, viewed the whole, differently. The fourth century saw a shift, as Christianity came first to challenge and then to replace that original classical vision, incorporating much of the cultural patrimony of the ancient world into its own understanding. From that time on Western civilization has been, to one degree or another, a set of Christendom societies. This does not mean that the majority of the members of such societies have been seriously committed Christians. It means that there was a general acceptance of basic Christian truths and an assumption of the Christian narrative and vision of the world around which the societies' institutions were gathered.

Again, to call such a society as this 'Christian' does not mean that the majority of its members were serious or educated Christians; in fact, there has probably never existed a human society for which that was the case. There is a reason why all the saints of Christendom have so constantly and urgently spoken out against the lack of genuine faith of their times. They were not unreasonable extremists holding to an overly rigorous standard, or romantic dreamers out of touch with human reality. Rather, they recognized that though the main institutions of their societies were under the influence of Christianity, there were always counter-currents running, and the majority of their members were far from living as convinced and serious Christians. They saw that much that went by the name Christian was in fact a watered-down reduction of it.

The presence of an assumed Christian vision goes far to explain why the preaching, in a Christendom context, of a Bernardino of Siena or a Vincent Farrar or a Savonarola or a John Wesley was so remarkably effective, with whole towns and cities embracing their message and social life (for a time) transformed. The overwhelming and immediate response to the proclamation of the preacher showed (apart from the grace of God) that his hearers shared his fundamental assumptions, which were present but often asleep within them. Their hearts resonated with an effective call to embrace the message more seriously, for it was the bringing alive of dormant truths, the making real of what was often only theoretical, the filling out of what had been reduced or corrupted.

In this regard it is instructive to observe the difference in the reception of the Gospel by various groups of people as recorded in the Acts of the Apostles. Three instances of preaching will show this principle in operation: Peter's preaching to the Jews just after Pentecost (Acts 2:14-42), the preaching of Paul and Barnabas to the pagan populace of the town of Lystra (Acts 14:8-18), and Paul's preaching to the Athenians at the Areopagus (Acts 17:22-32).

As to the first of these: the Jews were a religious people whose imaginative vision of the world was similar to Peter's, who was himself a believing Jew. They knew what he meant by 'God,' heaven and hell, sin and repentance, prophecy and providence, the Covenant and the Messiah. The proclamation of the Gospel added something of vital importance to the Jewish understanding, but it assumed and built upon an existing vision. Peter's words found resonance in the deep substratum of the minds of his hearers, and three thousand converted in one day. And once converted to faith in Christ, these new believers did not need to be brought to an entirely different way of seeing the world; rather, they could be welcomed into the newborn Church and take their places as intelligent believers fairly quickly. Even the opposition by some of the Jews to the preaching of the Gospel showed that they understood what was being said and knew what was at stake. A great deal could be taken for granted; the issue among them was simply whether or not this Jesus of Nazareth was indeed the promised Messiah. One sees a similar pattern in instances of Paul's preaching at Jewish synagogues or among God-fearers as recorded throughout the book of Acts. There was rapid understanding, and whether the message was embraced or rejected (or a mixture of both), it was not difficult for Paul to make himself understood by his hearers. The same could be said for Paul's own conversion. His ability to begin preaching Christianity so soon after he had recognized Christ as Messiah was based upon his grasp of the whole Jewish imaginative and narrative vision, one that the Christians had retained.

The reception of the ministry of Paul and Barnabas in the second instance tells a different story. Lystra seems to have been a believing pagan town where the Greek mythological vision of the world was ascendant. When Paul preached and then healed a crippled man, the crowds in the town were moved and impressed, but they interpreted what they saw and heard through the lens of their assumed pagan vision, and they became convinced that the gods, Zeus and Hermes, had come down among them in human form. Paul and Barnabas were appalled and could barely keep the multitude from offering sacrifice to them, a very different response than that of the Jews at Pentecost. If three thousand devout pagans such as these had been converted in one day, they would have had to undergo a far more profound transformation of mind than had the Jews in order to reasonably be called Christian.

Lastly, in the Areopagus Paul was dealing with yet another imaginative understanding of the world, one dominated by the philosophical schools to which Athens was the renowned home. Paul went at his task differently, in a way that could engage a sophisticated and philosophically critical vision of the cosmos. The response he received was in keeping with the assumptions of the environment: it was not nothing, but it was less immediate and enthusiastic than in either of the other two settings. Among some of his hearers an attitude of mockery arose which, although not surprising among the intellectually sophisticated and religiously skeptical, neither the believing Jews nor the Zeus-worshipping pagans exhibited.

We might then note these two basic modes by which Christianity interacts with human societies: an apostolic mode and a Christendom mode. The first is her way of confronting a society with a very different overall vision than her own; the second is her mode of acting when Christianity has fertilized the soil out of which the society's basic assumptions spring. Putting it this way is of course far too simplistic: human societies are dynamic, and the degree to which Christianity is formative of a society's culture and vision is never complete and never static. Nonetheless it can be of use to view these two modes as "ideal types" in order to inquire how best to respond to the cultural matrix we currently inhabit.

II

Christendom and Apostolic Modes: Advantages and Challenges

The Church does not feel dispensed from paying unflagging attention to those who have received the Faith and who have been in contact with the Gospel often for generations. Thus she seeks to deepen, consolidate, nourish and make ever more mature the faith of those who are already called the faithful or believers, in order that they may be so still more.

— POPE ST. PAUL VI, Evangelii Nuntiandi, 54

If Christianity, on one hand, has found its most effective form in Europe, it is necessary, on the other hand, to say that in Europe a culture has developed that constitutes the absolutely most radical contradiction not only of Christianity, but of the religious and moral traditions of humanity.

— POPE BENEDICT XVI, Subiaco Address

A CHRISTENDOM situation gives the Church certain advantages, but also brings with it certain challenges and opens the door to certain temptations. An apostolic or missionary situation does the same. The Church has negotiated both in many different places and times. The key is to understand one's own time and to develop a pastoral and evangelistic strategy appropriate to the prevailing spiritual and cultural environment. Before looking at what elements of such a strategy might be, it will help to delineate in greater detail these two ideal types.

Concerning a Christendom Culture

Christendom comes about due to the success of the Church's missionary activity in winning converts and in vivifying the wider culture. There is an obvious great good involved in a Christendom society. It can only be good that a human culture be brought into greater rather than lesser alignment with the truth and goodness of God. It can only be fitting that the Lord of heaven and earth be acknowledged as such and that signs of his presence and expressions of his rule be formative for human life. To the degree that a human society is founded on Christian truth and its members have willingly embraced that truth, and to the degree that their vision of the cosmos corresponds to the way God sees things, that society and the individuals within it have overcome ignorance and aligned themselves to reality.

In a Christendom culture, the primary need is maintenance, in the best sense of the word. In such times, Christianity holds the field in the key institutions of the society and dominates its grand narrative. Its task, in the words of Pope Paul VI quoted above, is "to deepen, consolidate, nourish and make ever more pure the faith of those who are already called believers." During such times the Church baptizes many societal institutions, founds others, and then struggles to maintain and deepen their influence. The task has never been an easy one; Christianity is not natural to a fallen world, and there are many forces, both human and spiritual, constantly at work to undermine and overthrow the influence of Christ upon humanity, individually and collectively. The tendency to reduce or assimilate the Gospel to non-Christian cultural beliefs and practices is a constant, corroding presence, unique to each time and place and often subtle in its operation. Too often, a society embraces many genuinely Christian elements and calls itself truly Christian, even while denying faith's heart. Fallen humans are always prone to idolize the visible while forgetting more important invisible realities. Christendom is not a societal state gained once for all but rather an ideal never fully achieved, one that needs renewing, strengthening, and correcting at every turn. To perform this task well has demanded its own kind of heroism, as all the saints of Christendom have made clear by their lives and teaching.

A Christendom society fosters great cultural achievements. In such times Christianity leaves its mark on institutions of education, law and government; it influences art, architecture and literature. As the Christian ideal gets into the soil of the society, remarkable cultural fertility results. Such a society will develop its institutions and expressions almost unconsciously, with a characteristic strength and unanimity that seems mysterious. It is difficult adequately to explain historically why, for example, slavery slowly disappeared in the West, or universities sprang up, or parliaments began to be developed. There is something mysterious in the way Gothic cathedrals were raised in city after city, or hospitals and orphanages and other charitable ventures sprouted like a natural growth, or villages grew as almost organic things out of the living rock, with a ruling spirit ever in evidence but often not explicit. These and countless other cultural developments were the outworking of deeply held cultural assumptions and an integrated vision of the cosmos that cultural leaders and artists and artisans intuited and brought into material and institutional form. And once founded, such institutions tended to great longevity and so could be developed over generations and centuries, gaining significant cultural depth and authority.

In a Christendom society fundamental law and basic moral understanding are rooted in Christian truth. This is an advantage for many reasons, not least for family life and the raising of children. With good example and good influence readily available and the stated ideals of the society clear — if not universally followed — Christians can count on the wider culture for basic support. What Christian parents are teaching their children at home will resonate with the ideals held out by the authorities of the society. For those who grow up under its influence, a Christian vision will tend to become part of the furniture of the mind. As the fundamentals of the Faith become first principles of thought and behavior, there comes to prevail an instinctive resonance with Christian truth for which there will hardly be need to argue.

In Christendom, believers are fundamentally at peace as regards their faith. Although peacefulness can encourage complacency, there is nonetheless an objective good in living peacefully, worshiping freely, and founding and developing institutions that honor Christ without constant battle. The hostility of a darkened world is to some degree kept at bay.

In Christendom, the blessings of God's government are scattered abroad, allowing a certain goodness to pervade the whole of the society. Despite the many sins and failings of Christians, the presence of Christ sweetens human life. People are generally happier.

Nonetheless, Christendom also brings with it stiff challenges, due in part to its successes. When Christianity becomes the main cultural current, many tend to be lukewarm in their pursuit of their faith, more or less going along for the ride. Christian devotion can become conventional, losing its radical character and thus its dynamism and attractiveness. The great sin of Christendom is hypocrisy, pretending to be more interested in God and in virtue than one is.

Professing Christianity is the norm; living the Faith as a genuine disciple is the exception.

As a result, a distinction arises between the nominal and the seriously committed Christian that is not found in the first age of the Church's life. In a Christendom society the level of Christian transformation expected of the general populace is rather low, and many who desire seriously to serve Christ feel that they must do something decisive to express the true Christian spirit, usually by entering a religious order. In Christendom ages this has sometimes been called "leaving the world," as if all Christians were not supposed to leave the "world" in the scriptural meaning of the word. A sense of first- and second-class members of the Church can develop, and the expectation of holiness among the laity can wane.

In a Christendom culture the Church as a whole is tempted to lose its spiritual and otherworldly character and to become merely a this-worldly body, a department of state or a promising career path, a center of civilized activities rather than the mystical body of Christ. Because in a Christendom society to profess Christ leads to respectability and can bring power and wealth, because Christ is a name to conjure with and by which to gain influence, greedy and power-hungry people prey upon the Church and use its influence to further their own selfish aims. Sins of buying Church offices, of absentee bishops and priests, of avarice and the hoarding of wealth, of a general creeping worldliness among those whose task it is to lead others to Christ can become rampant. Even for those who avoid such glaring sins, the message of Christ can become overlaid with the categories of success originating in the temporal order and can cease to be a liberating force. Priesthood can become merely a job rather than a mission. Attending to the moral and ritual life of the Church can become perfunctory, valued only for immediately tangible effects. This is the sort of concern that sparked the reforming spirit of the sixteenth century, both Protestant and Catholic. To reform the Church truly in such times is no easy task.

In Christendom, because institutions are strong and well-founded, they tend to be taken for granted and therefore to lose their originating Christian spirit. Bishops and priests can cease to operate as pastors and evangelists engaged in a high-stakes spiritual struggle who are using their institutions to lead their people to discipleship, and instead they can come to see themselves and function as system managers who keep the machine well-oiled. In a Christendom culture, the type of person who is brought forward to lead the Church is often the conflict-avoiding administrator rather than the apostle. The Church goes from being a movement of spirit incarnated in institutions to a set of sclerotic institutions that have lost their inner spirit.

In a Christendom society, the very strength of Christian institutions and principles brings a tendency to reduce the Faith to its visible expressions. Christians can wrongly think that the kingdom of heaven is fundamentally of this world, that its strength can be measured by its visible manifestations. As a result, they too often attempt to maintain worldly influence at the expense of genuine spiritual strength. The story, perhaps apocryphal, of an encounter of Saint John Vianney and the devil is expressive of the true source of the Church's influence. The devil is said to have told Vianney that if there were three such priests as he, the kingdom of darkness would be ruined. Holiness, prayer, humility, hidden acts of charity are the spiritual means by which the Church is visibly upheld. When these are diminished, the outward expressions of the Church's life grow tenuous and liable to failure. The Church is never in a more fragile situation than when she seems strong but has lost her deep rootedness in the invisible world. This danger can be hard to see in a Christendom age.

More subtly, in a Christendom time there are often counterfeits of genuine Christianity that assimilate Christian names and customs to what is in fact a different religion. John Henry Newman has noted this phenomenon in a sermon entitled "Religion of the Day":

> In every age of Christianity, since it was first preached, there has been what may be called a *religion of the world*, which so far imitates the one true religion, as to deceive the unstable and unwary. The world does not oppose religion *as such.* I may say, it never has opposed it. In particular, it has, in all ages, acknowledged in one sense or other the Gospel of Christ, fastened on one or other of its characteristics, and professed to embody this in its practice; while by neglecting the other parts of the holy doctrine, it has, in fact, distorted and corrupted even that portion of it which it has exclusively put forward, and so has contrived to explain away the whole; — for he who cultivates only one precept of the Gospel to the exclusion of the rest, in reality attends to no part at all. (Plain & Parochial Sermons, Vol 1, #24)

This substitution of the part for the whole can result in confusion concerning who Christ is and what his Gospel demands. Many who have accepted a distorted understanding of the Faith will claim to speak in Christ's name.

Because in a Christendom society the whole of the population (nearly) is Christian, the imperative for mission can wane. The truth that the human race is caught up in a cosmic battle between good and evil in which each individual needs to declare for one side or the other can be effectively hidden. For many living in a Christendom time, the Church can be seen as one among many cultural institutions that enhance human life, rather than as the re-created human race saved from death and slavery. Mission then becomes the preserve of a few religious orders laboring in lands far away. The Great Commission can seem a distant and irrelevant command.

Concerning an Apostolic Time

In an apostolic situation, because the Church is not the major influence in the society's overarching vision, the need is not mainly for maintenance, though this comes into play; it is rather for apostolic witness and the building of a distinctively Christian cultural vision and way of life. In such a time the Church understands herself to be vastly different from the world around her, needing to make her way against hostility or apathy, unable to count on the wider society to sustain her institutions or to carry her vision of life. Such a cultural stance also brings with it certain advantages, as well as certain challenges.

Because one has to pay a serious price for the Faith in an apostolic time, there is less hypocrisy than in a Christendom age. The life of faith is more intense and therefore more attractive, more evidently life-changing. There is an immediate experience of the momentousness of belonging to Christ. The great adventure of Christianity is more palpable: its contours show up with greater clarity, and the Gospel attracts many high-hearted people who have a strong desire for God and for goodness. The specifically Christian quality of the lives of believers tends to be higher.

In an apostolic age there is by necessity greater purity of intention in priests and bishops, which makes for truer and more dynamic leadership. A higher standard of holiness among the clergy is more natural and easier to sustain. Those who might pursue Church offices for money or social prestige will usually find something else to do.

In an apostolic age the Church is in a sense more self-conscious. Christians know by daily experience that they inhabit a spiritual and moral world different from and often in opposition to the one around them, and this demands a greater sense of their distinct call. In an apostolic age every Christian is by necessity a witness and an evangelist; the role of the laity and the importance of lay holiness emerge with greater clarity as necessary for the Church to complete her mission.

Confessing Christ in the face of hostility even to the point of martyrdom has always been accounted the greatest of Christian blessings, the most privileged way to imitate Christ, but it is hard to come by in a Christendom age. In an apostolic age the possibility of suffering for the Faith, even undergoing martyrdom, is present, as a heroic spirit of witnessing with courage animates the whole of the Church.

There are also challenges that come with an apostolic age. The various benefits that accrue in a Christendom culture are not present. Error in all its forms, doctrinal and moral, is rife. In such a cultural atmosphere it can be difficult for Christians to sustain their own spiritual and moral vision. Material advantages are offered to those who make peace with the non-Christian majority, and the attractiveness of the ruling vision is hard to resist, especially for the most vulnerable. Among other problems, it becomes more difficult to raise children in the Faith.

In an apostolic age the hostility of the wider culture can make a settled life difficult. Institutions are harder to found and harder to keep healthy, like trying to build a house in a gale wind. Fewer resources are available, and the cultural challenge of articulating the Faith, both individually and institutionally, can be exhausting. Especially among those who measure the strength of the Church by her visible manifestations, there can be a tendency to discouragement and a waning of confidence in the power of the Gospel.

Precisely because of the high cost of discipleship, the great temptation in an apostolic age is not to hypocrisy but to cowardice. While in Christendom people are tempted to profess more faith and virtue than they possess, in an apostolic age they are tempted to profess less. Open apostasy motivated by fear becomes more common.

In an apostolic age, because of the bitterness of the spiritual climate, groups of Christians face the temptation to develop an overly rigoristic attitude to faith and the moral life or to become sectarian and abandon the task of engaging and confronting the wider culture with the Gospel. There can be a tendency to "let the rest of the world go to hell" or to become dominated by a fearful attitude that robs the Gospel of its joyful and conquering spirit. Recognizing that there is a line of demarcation between Christianity and the wider society, the temptation arises to set that line in places not demanded by the Gospel. Just as accommodation to this-worldly currents of thought and behavior is the besetting temptation of many in a Christendom age, so the erecting of personal or group orthodoxies that do not map onto the true lines of the Gospel is the temptation of many in an apostolic age.

III

The Current Climate

> Even in countries evangelized many centuries ago, the reality of a 'Christian society' which, amid all the frailties which have always marked human life, measured itself explicitly on Gospel values, is now gone.
>
> — POPE ST. JOHN PAUL II, *Novo Millenio Ineunte*, 40

WHATEVER THE advantages and disadvantages of a Christendom or an apostolic cultural situation may be, we do not get to choose the sort of society we would prefer. We receive from Christ both the times in which we are to live and the grace to engage our world as it is. As we turn our eyes to our own time and place and ask what kind of culture we inhabit, what its overarching imaginative vision is and what the pastoral strategies appropriate to it are, we open upon a complex and in many respects unprecedented picture. Living in this unprecedented complexity requires new and effective ways of living the Gospel and of witnessing to the truths of the Faith.

The last several centuries have seen an increasingly bitter contest in the West between two competing ruling visions: a largely Christian vision that had pertained for many centuries, and a humanistic and materialistic vision that began to emerge in the latter part of the seventeenth century, which goes by the general name of 'the Enlightenment.' To say that these two visions have been in conflict is not to say that they share nothing in common or that the earlier Christian vision has not been a source of much in the Enlightenment one. But although these two visions might view *some* things similarly, they view *everything* differently; the overall scheme or pattern into which various beliefs or practices are embedded gives a different meaning even to that which — taken separately — might be similar.

Until around World War I, Europe was by and large a set of Christendom cultures, though insightful observers were seeing the direction toward which it was headed much earlier. For there had been a kind of cultural civil war being fought for close to two hundred years, with greater or lesser intensity, especially among the educated classes. In the century since, that war is essentially over in Europe; Christendom has been chased from the field — not Christianity or the Church, but Europe as a Christendom society. By contrast, America has until very recently been a kind of Christendom culture, and in some places, it remains so to a significant degree. From its beginnings, the American societal vision was something of an alloy. In an uneasy mix, there was a smelting of Christian elements inherited from the long history of the West with elements of the Enlightenment. That American cultural vision has been on the whole friendly to Christianity, but that is rapidly dissipating. Many recent developments make this clear. The change runs deep, and it is not likely to be reversed anytime soon.

The point of recounting all this is not to announce apocalypse nor to indulge in nostalgia. Rather, it is to suggest that we need to understand our culture — its darkest depths as well as its most promising aspects — so that we can begin to know how to bring the light of Christ to it.

Thinking with a Christendom Mode in an Apostolic Time

Not surprisingly, there are many American Catholics who still have a Christendom mentality. They were raised with it, and it has become part of the assumed furniture of their minds. This inherited attitude is understandable, but from a strategic point of view, it is also disastrous. The rapid change from a Christendom ruling vision to a modern progressive utopian one has radically altered the strategic situation.

In this regard it would be well to take note of places like Quebec, Belgium, Spain, and Ireland. Until recently, the culture in these places appeared to be soundly Catholic even while the wider world was embracing a secular orientation. Yet in the space of one generation the bottom of the Christendom culture fell out. Almost overnight, these societies went from being strongly Catholic to aggressively secular. One reason for the rapid collapse was that the overarching vision of the society had been changing over a course of time, but the change was not perceived and the institutions of the Church were not adjusting to it; they rather continued to be led under an attitude of "business as usual." At a certain point the eroding Christian vision could no longer bear the weight of the culture; the house collapsed, and great was its fall. These admittedly complex situations point to a working principle: institutional and ecclesiastical strategies that are suited to Christendom do not work well in an apostolic setting. During a time when there is rapid change away from a Christendom vision, a time like our own, the Church needs to think about the spirit and operation of all of her institutions in a different way. Otherwise, those institutions could lose their effectiveness or be captured by the prevailing culture.

Under a different set of cultural conditions, a similar changing of a culture's ruling narrative vision can be seen to be at work in Latin

America. This region has long been made up of a set of Christendom societies, whose overarching vision has been carried by the Catholic Church. For the past hundred years or so, however, that imaginative vision has been under serious attack, first from aggressively secular governments and more recently through electronic media and economic factors connecting its users to a largely secular global culture. Older institutional and cultural formulations developed during those Christendom years are not working as well as they once did. Nonetheless, the great majority of Latin Americans still identify as Christian. But while the Catholic Church has been losing numbers and influence among Latin populations, Protestant Evangelical Christianity has seen a sharp rise. Whatever the limitations of that stream of Christianity may be, it goes forward, evangelistically and pastorally, under an apostolic mode. It assumes a mission posture and is therefore better suited to address the current Latin situation. The more that Latin American Catholics embrace apostolicity, the less likely their congregations and their families will be to abandon their faith, whether to the secular global culture or to small independent churches. To the degree that they continue with "business as usual," they can expect to watch an ever-increasing number of their members go elsewhere.

Here in the United States we can see this principle working itself out in all the key institutions of the Church: the family, schools, charity organizations, parishes, chanceries. Older patterns and institutional strategies that worked well in their time no longer catch the ear of the culture or maintain their hold on members of the Church. The children of Catholic parents often leave the Faith; Catholic schools and universities do not graduate serious Catholic believers; parishes do not produce vocations to the priesthood and religious life; religious orders shrivel. For those with a Christendom orientation, the news of our time is one long tale of decline and loss: numbers down, institutions secularized or moribund, loss of cultural clout evident. All this can produce an atmosphere of discouragement and defeatism.

Alongside this picture needs to be placed another and more encouraging one. Wherever apostolic zeal and apostolic strategies are in operation, the results are impressive: one sees conversions to the Faith, especially among the young; new movements and religious communities being born or rediscovering their vitality; institutions being founded or reformed; a deepening life of prayer and communal witness being expressed. These movements do not involve majorities, but that is part of the nature of an apostolic time: in a mission setting, the Church does not move by majorities. What we face is not a culture so corrupt that it is immune to the Gospel nor a populace for whom Catholicism has altogether lost its bite or its attractiveness. Our problem is rather that much of the Church is still in a Christendom mode, either seriously compromised by the ruling vision of the wider culture or using outmoded strategies that were devised for a different context, and so it is unable to cope with the current culture. The task at hand is to find ways successfully to engage members in the Church — and those outside of it — with the truths of the Faith.

There is a telling event in the life of the prophet Elisha, recounted in the Second Book of Kings (6:23-8). An alliance of hostile powers had invaded Israel, and an army was laying siege to the city where Elisha was staying with his servant. In this dire predicament the servant grew anxious, but Elisha encouraged him with the words, "Don't be afraid; those who are with us are more than those who are with them." This made no sense to the servant, who could see no allies but only a vast army of enemies. So Elisha prayed that the servant's eyes would be opened to see the spiritual world, to catch a glimpse of the genuine reality. The young man's eyes were opened, and he saw an army of heavenly horsemen and chariots around Elisha more than equal to the task of handling the enemy forces. This is not just a charming story; it is the expression of a truth of great practical importance. The Church will regularly appear to be the underdog when an assessment of her fortunes looks only at the visible world of politics, economics, cultural clout, and numbers. But when the Church is seen truly, as a divine society transcending space and time, filled with the presence and strength of God, resplendent with the power and beauty of angels and perfected humans, bringing all the authority of heaven to bear on the world's affairs, the picture looks quite different. An apostolic age, especially one now emerging from the ruins of a Christendom culture, needs to be clear about the sources of the Church's strength in the battles she faces.

IV

Devising a Pastoral Strategy for this Transitional Time

> As I have said on other occasions, the new and unique situation in which the world and the Church find themselves at the threshold of the Third Millennium, and the urgent needs which result, mean that the mission of evangelization today calls for a new program which can be defined overall as a 'new evangelization.'
>
> — POPE ST. JOHN PAUL II, Ecclesia in America, 243

> Modern man listens more willingly to witnesses than to teachers, and if he does listen to teachers, it is because they are witnesses.
>
> — POPE ST. PAUL VI, Evangelii Nuntiandi, 41

IN LIGHT of these considerations, what are some principles and attitudes upon which to formulate a reasonable pastoral and evangelistic response?

1. Gaining an apostolic attitude

The first requisite is to note the times in which we live and to be ready to adjust expectations and strategies accordingly. In this regard we might begin by considering the apostles soon after the ascension of Christ. They had been newly filled with the power of the Holy Spirit and had the words of their resurrected Master ringing in their ears: "Go and make disciples of all nations." This was the quintessential apostolic situation. One can imagine them gathering for their first "evangelization committee meeting."

Our Agenda

To bring the Gospel of Christ to the world.

Our Resources

Bishops? . . . . Eleven.

Priests? . . . . Same number.

Deacons? . . . . None.

Trained theologians? . . . . None.

Religious orders? . . . . None.

Seminarians? . . . . None.

Seminaries? . . . . None.

Christian believers? . . . . A few hundred.

Countries with Christians in them? . . . . One.

Church buildings? . . . . None.

Schools and universities? . . . . None.

Written Gospels? . . . . None.

Money? . . . . Very little.

Experience in foreign missions? . . . . None.

Influential contacts in high places? . . . . Next to none.

Societal attitude toward us? . . . . Ignorant to hostile.

If the Apostles had been thinking in a Christendom mode and had assessed their situation from the standpoint of the strength of existing Christian institutions, they would have been overwhelmed by discouragement, facing crises in every direction: vocational, financial, catechetical, educational, and numerical. But they weren't discouraged; they were filled with joy and hope. They had great confidence in their Lord, in their message, and in the creativity and fertility of the Church. They knew that their task was to be used by the Holy Spirit to grow the Church, and they knew the graced means by which it was to grow. And grow it did.

The Church in an apostolic time needs to have the same confidence in the power and goodness of the message she bears, in its life-changing potency, in the Church's power of regeneration and growth. In a particular way, those in positions of influence and authority need to be convinced that Christ is the answer to every human ill, the solution to every human problem, the only hope for a dying race. They need to be convinced of the bad news: that the human race has by its own rebellion brought a curse upon itself and has sold itself into slavery to the prince of darkness, and there is nothing we can do under our own power to save ourselves. At the same time, they need to be equally convinced of the Good News: that God in his mercy has come among us to set us free from our sins and from slavery to the devil, and for those who turn to their true allegiance, the nightmare of life apart from God can be transformed into a dawn of eternal hope. They need to know, from their own experience, that obedience to the Gospel is perfect freedom, that holiness leads to happiness, that a world without God is a desolate wasteland, and that new life in Christ transforms darkness into light.

This attitude, necessary for many reasons, is essential for properly evaluating the Church's work and fortunes in a post-Christendom age. In a time of transition such as ours, we should expect that the pastoral and evangelistic strategies that have pertained for a long time under the influence of an assumed Christendom narrative vision will no longer prove as effective as they once did. We should expect that many who have attended Mass because it was the conventional thing to do will stop attending and that those who have no real conviction about the truths of the Faith will be reluctant to pay a high price for those truths and will increasingly keep their distance. There are many "hereditary Catholics" currently in the Church, who have sentimental ties to the way in which they were raised. But sentimentality will not sustain a way of discipleship that will challenge them at every level of their being, nor will it sustain their faith when it brings them into conflict with those around them. We ought not be cavalier about this or quick to quench the smoldering wick, however weak the flame has become; every soul, no matter how tepid, is of immense importance. But the fundamental task of the Church, one that can get lost under a Christendom mentality, needs to be kept in view.

Old Simeon, holding the child Jesus in the Temple, spoke of him as being the fall and the rise of many in Israel and the instrument whereby hearts would be tested (Lk 2:34). The great task of the Church in every age is to preach and live the Gospel with clarity and conviction; what effect that may have on others is not hers to determine. Jesus, the greatest and most talented preacher of the Gospel in history, did not gain a good reception from all his hearers; sometimes even a majority rejected his message. This was not because his preaching, to the extent that it did not produce conversion, failed. Rather, it succeeded perfectly in what it was meant to do: it tested the hearts of those hearing such that they either rose or fell when confronted by his message. The same is true in the Church's witness to the Faith. However faithfully Christ is presented, the response to the Gospel will be mixed. There is no getting around the fact that, in a society moving away from Christendom, the Church will by a kind of social necessity grow smaller: the majority in any society tends to embrace the ruling societal vision unconsciously unless they explicitly move out of it to something else. This needs, however, to be seen in proper perspective. Ten genuine followers of Christ will prove more fecund in new believers than a thousand whose faith is lukewarm or non-existent. The Church does not grow by mass movement; it moves forward one soul at a time, as each individual catches the fire of belief from another and is grafted into the body of Christ. The importance is not found in numbers but in the intensity of the flame, as the Apostles understood.

2. Refusing to be trapped by social analysis

An apostolic age needs to free itself from the logic of sociological surveys and numerical extrapolations about the place of belief in the coming age. Whatever their use, such things tell us very little about the future fortunes of the Church. They leave out faith and miracle and the Holy Spirit by a necessity of their method, and so they will necessarily be inaccurate concerning the activity of a spiritual organism with its roots in heaven. What sociological survey could have predicted the conversion of an ancient and sophisticated civilization at the hands of a small group of uneducated laborers? What numerical analysis could have surmised the explosion of the monastic movement? Or the conversion of all the pagan peoples of Europe? Or the appearance of a Saint Francis and his thousands of followers in a few short years? Or the apparition of Our Lady of Guadalupe and the conversion of Mexico? Or, for that matter, the conversion of a single soul? What sociological study can gauge the presence of the Holy Spirit or the power of prayer? From its first appearance, the Church has been a massive surprise; in every age its existence is a standing miracle. The unlikely and unlooked-for success of Christianity tends to get lost in a Christendom culture, when the wonder and the revolutionary power of an Incarnate God can come to be seen as just part of the way things are supposed to go. But in every age the Church runs counter to the spiritual atmosphere of a darkened world, even if at times it is successful enough to influence that atmosphere in significant ways. Every conversion is a marvel of grace, an astonishing work of God. Saint Augustine once said that it was a greater miracle for God to save one sinner than to have created the whole world. Augustine's comment points to the attitude appropriate to an apostolic age.

This is not to say that such societal analyses are of no worth or should be ignored. They are useful, even essential, in helping Christians to understand the culture they are navigating, and they can provide necessary information concerning the current state of belief. They can be used as spurs to action and as information to construct the appropriate stance and strategy of the Church. But sociological analyses are not markers of the Church's spiritual strength, nor can they predict how the Church will fare into the future, nor should they be a source of hand-wringing and an excuse for lack of faith.

As an example, in the late eighteenth century the European Church was in a general state of lassitude, with large numbers of its educated classes falling off from their faith. Then came the French Revolution, and Christendom's lead country was thrown into twenty-five years of warfare, chaos, and waves of forced dechristianization. The Pope was for a time held prisoner, the traditional Christian monarchies were tottering, and many thought the Church was on her last legs: old, lacking conviction, about to expire. Vocations to the priesthood and religious life in France were at a very low ebb, seminary instruction was lacking, many religious orders had lost their foundations, and there were contrary ideals and currents of unbelief in the wider society set against Christianity and the Church that weren't likely to go away. A sympathetic observer of the state of the French church around the year 1810 or 1815 would have seen nothing but wreckage and, given simple sociological data, would have predicted vocational disaster into the future with everything that implies. What happened was something different. In 1808 there were 12,300 religious sisters in France. In 1878 there were 135,000. In 1830 there were some 3,000 priests of all kinds serving the French Church. In 1878 there were around 30,000, a ten-fold increase in sixty years, and their median age in 1878 was significantly younger than it had been sixty years earlier. Whatever might be said of the Church's fortunes at that time, it was evident that it wasn't about to disappear. All of this was a great surprise to the Church's enemies, especially to those who were developing the discipline of sociology as a kind of replacement for theology and who were happily predicting, under its methodology, the demise of the Church. According to their logic, none of this should have happened. The point is that the Church has great powers of regeneration. It is not a static body with a fixed amount of resources and a limited number of adherents. It responds to each situation it encounters with the power and the generative quality of the Holy Spirit. This regeneration happens when the members of the Church take stock of their times, renew their commitment to the whole of the Gospel, and place themselves at the service of Christ. Of course, if the Church and the Faith are treated as purely human constructs, numerical analyses will have more predictive power, and the common dire prognostications are then more likely to come true.

3. Maintaining and using institutions differently

A key difference between a Christendom and an apostolic age has to do with the way Church institutions function. Institutions are essential to Church life, indeed to human life. They are a necessity of existence in a world of space and time. It is no surprise then that in God's dealings with the human race, he has been so insistent on the founding and maintenance of proper institutions within which humans can live and their ideals and relationships can come to fruition. The family is the primeval human institution, and the Church is the most important and most comprehensive institution of all, the home in which the whole person is addressed and cared for into eternity. And there are a host of other institutions in between, from parishes, to schools, religious orders, charity organizations, businesses and neighborhood associations, which together provide the fabric of a healthy life.

The word "institution," although it has a long and illustrious Christian pedigree, currently has a stodgy and impersonal feel, and we can be reluctant to use it. This reluctance is due partly to the way the word has been used in sociological analysis. But it is also due to the sad fact that most modern institutions have for various reasons become corrupted and therefore inhuman places. A healthy institution is always ordered to the human person and enhances, or at least does not diminish, the humanity of those under its influence. When we think of an institution, the first thing that should come to mind is not an overly-bureaucratized business or a forbidding school building, much less a prison, but rather a close-knit family circle or a parish where faith and love are evident and all are well cared for. When Christian institutions have lost much of their spirit and freshness, it becomes tempting to think that the solution is to be found in leaving institutions behind altogether. "Spirituality" comes to replace "organized religion," by which is meant religion seated in institutions. The incarnation of religious ideals in institutions, an essential operation in God's providential plan of salvation, is perceived as inimical to vibrant faith. Given the current cultural confusion and the subjectivist nature of our time, this is an understandable mistake, but it is a serious mistake nonetheless. Properly founding and caring for institutions in which the ideals of a culture are incarnated is the heart of all civilized life. God is very much in favor of (proper) institutions, as is clear by his founding them and his insistence on their maintenance. Jesus spent much of his time among his closest disciples, laying the groundwork for the institution that he himself would inhabit by the Holy Spirit.

It seems a law of institutional life that a given institution will tend to conform to the overarching imaginative and moral vision of the society in which it finds itself. When that ruling vision is a good one, such conformity is an advantage. When it is Christian, it is an especial advantage; one of the advantages of a Christendom society is exactly this tendency for its institutions to take a Christian form. But this comes with a corollary: a Christian institution in a non-Christian or anti-Christian cultural environment can only maintain its distinctively Christian character by energetic resistance to conformity with the wider atmosphere. Not to exercise such concerted activity is to lose the institution's original purpose. In other words, for a Christian institution to shed its Christian bearings and spirit in an apostolic time, whether the institution be a family or a parish or a university or a charity organization, it does not need to be led decisively away from Christianity. All it needs to do is carry on in a maintenance "business as usual" mode, and in a fairly short space of time, as the institution conforms to dominant cultural forces, its inner spirit will have been lost to Christ. It is the difference between floating a canoe downriver with the occasional guiding push (in Christendom mode) or steering it upriver against the current with energetic strokes (in apostolic mode). What happens when the rowing stops is quite different in the two cases. Those who think the current is going their way — when in fact it is against them — will be surprised to find themselves rushing along in a direction they did not intend.

In an apostolic time, institutions need to become more self-conscious about their mission, their aims, and their inner spirit. Those who lead and inhabit them need to know with greater clarity what they are doing, why they are doing it, what the likely consequences of taking certain kinds of decisions will be, and how the inner culture of the institution is best maintained against the tide.

What is needed here can be seen clearly in the current marriage culture. Not so long ago — in fact, only a generation or two ago — it was sufficient for a young Christian couple who wanted to marry and raise a family to do so according to the way they had been raised, following the general stream of the culture. They knew there were some societal patterns they would want to avoid, but there was a fairly clear path ahead of them. Many such couples would not have been able to articulate in any detail why they lived the way they did, raised and educated their children in a given way, pursued their work and recreational life according to a certain pattern. It was the obvious thing to do in a Christendom culture; it had long been done this way; it did not need to be spoken about; it had worked for their parents, and it would work for them. But in the current climate, the results of the inadequacy of this way of proceeding are evident on every side. How often parents of a certain age mourn the loss of their children to the Faith without knowing how or why it happened. "We sent them to Catholic schools; we took them to Mass. We did everything our own parents did! What went wrong?" A way of living Catholic family life that would have been at least adequate in a Christendom culture is now sadly inadequate to compete with the overpowering atmosphere that their children inhabit.

In the current cultural climate young, serious-minded Christians who marry are much clearer about their task. From the start, their decisions to get married at all, to remain chaste before marriage, to intend their marriage to last for life, and to welcome children into their family have put them into a counter-cultural stance, one that will be viewed as strange by many of their peers. They know they will have to think through every aspect of their family's life if they are to maintain its Christian vitality. They understand that they will not be able to depend on the wider culture as a pattern for how they should raise or educate their children, or how they should spend their money, or use technology, or choose among entertainment options. They are aware of the need for an integrated vision of their institutional (family) life within which all its activities can find meaning. They will need to raise their children differently from how they themselves were raised, not necessarily because their parents did a bad job, but because the surrounding environment has so radically changed. They are consciously moving from a Christendom mode of thinking and acting to an apostolic one. They know that their family life, if properly established, will not only provide a good environment for their children but will also be a source of intrigue and hope to many around them looking for a better way to live. Raising a Christian family has always been a serious task; in an apostolic age, it is a missionary adventure.

In other Church institutions — schools, universities, charities, and parishes — the same principle is at work. Such institutions will cease to be meaningfully Christian and Catholic unless there is clarity of identity and understanding concerning the aims of the institution among all its members. In a Christendom age, an institution that is being led in a sleepy or muddled way will still be more or less Christian, riding the general drift of the culture. In an apostolic age, it will be rapidly swept down the current away from Christ and the Church. Because of this current danger, such institutions need to be more selective about whom they employ and more intentional about how they train their members. Those accustomed to functioning in a Christendom mode, or those who have lost the Christian narrative and have been largely captured by the overall vision of the wider culture, will no doubt find this difficult: it will seem doctrinaire, rigoristic, or intolerant. They have become accustomed to floating with the current, and the energy and clarity needed to navigate upstream is alien to them. Rather than taking as their pattern the whole Gospel of Christ in all its difficult and liberating clarity, they will tend to embrace less decisive formulations of their mission that allow compromise with the culture's ruling spirit. Vague talk about values will come to replace doctrine, Church liturgy, and discipleship — a recipe for losing the institution's founding ideals. Of course, those establishing or re-invigorating an institution need to be careful not to become sectarian or paranoid, ruled by fear rather than by faith. But they will also need to be clear and decisive.

The difference in attitude between institutions in a Christendom environment and institutions in an apostolic setting is highlighted by two of Jesus' pastoral teachings. In a Christendom setting, "he that is not against you is for you" (Luke 9:50). In Christendom, as long as there is no active opposition to the ideals of the institution, a certain number of apathetic or poorly trained members will do it no special harm. They will tend to conform, at least passively, to the Christendom orientation of the wider culture, and while they won't help move things forward or deepen their clarity, they won't get in the way. In an apostolic situation, "he who is not with me is against me, and he who does not gather with me scatters" (Luke 11:23). It is not enough in such a time to have a neutral or noncommittal attitude toward the aims of the institution in question. This supposed neutrality is not really neutral and will eventually result in active opposition, because such uncommitted members will likely conform to the wider societal vision without thinking about it. Whether they intend to or not, they will be adding their weight to the dissolution of the institution by the gradual eroding of its original purpose.

In a time like ours, a typical error of Church institutions is simply to avoid paying attention to questions of overall vision, to assume that such matters are either unimportant or are more or less settled, and to limit themselves to technical and administrative goals. Such goals may be praiseworthy or at least necessary, but they can become a distraction if they are pursued apart from deeper questions. In ignoring foundational matters and pursuing lesser ones, they can undermine the spirit of the institution. Given the current climate, the result may be institutions that possess various technical excellences but which will not be Christian.

For example, it is an aspect of the current cultural climate (and an unfortunate expression of its fundamental decadence) that technique and procedure are seen as the most important considerations for accomplishing serious goals. Unfortunately, this attitude can be taken on by those responsible for Catholic institutions. Rather than emphasizing the deepest questions — What is the good, the true, and the just? How can we develop the truly and fully human? What is expected of us by God? What will most conduce to eternal as well as temporal human happiness? — our society asks only: What is "best practice"? What is going to bring the highest return? What is the latest trend? What will most conform to the going professional standards? What will gain for us the greatest measure of social and professional prestige? What will be most immediately successful in a quantifiable, measurable mode? These are often important questions, but they can be answered well only when they are embedded in and ruled by more significant principles. Otherwise one can find that an alleged "best practice" may be damaging the human dignity of those using it, or that the latest pedagogical breakthrough may be founded on an anthropology that assumes a secular and unbelieving vision of humanity and thereby tends to destroy the faith of those under its influence, or that insisting on professionalism or respectability may in a given instance mean betraying the Gospel of Christ, or that pursuing profit alone will result in the subversion of the real purpose of the institution.

4. Establishing and strengthening practices that incarnate the Christian vision

In order for the unseen, spiritual world to become a living force in our minds, this invisible world needs to be visibly incarnated in space and time. This principle touches on the sacramental nature of things, the intercommunion between the material and the spiritual, and can be seen in the way God has revealed himself from the beginning. In showing himself to be the creator, the center of all being, the helper and redeemer of humanity, he did not merely get these ideas going esoterically in peoples' minds. He fashioned these invisible truths into visible forms that would be reminders of them and roads to experiencing them. Hence, he arranged for the Temple and its sacrifice, the Law, the Sabbath, the formation of a distinct people, the whole manner of life and worship that he gave to the Israelites. Finally, this principle of the invisible manifesting in the visible took definitive form in the coming of the incarnate Word of

God. Ever since then it has been expressed in a thousand ways by the Church. While faith is far more than its outward forms, without those forms it cannot long survive.

What has been true of the Church is true universally. Every society, seemingly by an inner law of its nature, expresses its ruling vision in a set of institutions and practices within which its ideas and principles clothe themselves. In this way the ruling vision comes to live in the minds and imaginations, as well as the physical and temporal environments, of its members. The things we do, the kind and manner of activities we engage in, the way we organize our lives, the way we structure the physical world around us, how we order our time, all will have a great deal to do with what we think and believe. The statement "out of sight, out of mind" is a popular way of getting at this. Ideas that are not incarnated in the stuff of the world soon lose their hold on our minds. This principle is of special importance for Christians. Christianity involves the revelation of a world that is largely invisible, most importantly concerning the being of God, but also including immortal human souls, angelic beings, humanity's true home in heaven, and a coming judgment. If these invisible realities are not incarnated in visible form, they will soon weaken their hold on the mind and imagination.

In a Christendom time, the Christian vision is the primary influence in shaping the "architecture" of the society as a whole. Not only church buildings and worship services but the organization of towns, the "soundscape" of bells, the division of the year by feasts and seasons, the way of working and dressing and eating and speaking, all express the invisible world behind the visible one. If that Christendom world is no longer present and the society is going in a different direction, Christians will need to find ways to create a societal architecture that incarnates an increasingly counter-cultural Christian vision.

Our current society, once visibly ordered to Christianity, has been transformed; it now incarnates a very different vision undergirded by a very different set of principles. It has largely forgotten the invisible world, such that its rhythms and practices are bounded by the visible and the temporal. Those under its influence will naturally have a hard time maintaining a clear sense of invisible and eternal realities. They will come to believe what they see and practice. A soldier on tour and away from his home will put a photograph of his wife and young children in a place of prominence as a way of keeping his affection and constancy fresh and vivid. Similarly, an individual Christian and the Church as a whole will find ways to express the invisible world around them, embodied in practices and customs, lest that vision first recede to the surface of their minds and finally be lost to them. This does not mean, for most, constructing an entirely different social and cultural world. It means learning to shake free of some of the secular practices around us, creatively finding ways to remind ourselves of the world as it truly is. Adjustments can be made around the ordering of our time, the arrangement of our homes, and the use of various electronic technologies, all directed toward constructing a genuine incarnation of a positive and coherent Christian vision of the world.

Liturgy takes on great importance in this regard as the focal point, the seed crystal, of the visible incarnation of invisible reality. Vatican II's document on liturgy, *Sacrosanctum Concilium*, puts the broad principle this way:

> It is of the essence of the Church that she be both human and divine, visible and yet invisibly equipped, eager to act and yet intent on contemplation, present in this world and yet not at home in it; and she is all these things in such wise that in her the human is directed and subordinated

> to the divine, the visible likewise to the invisible, action to contemplation, and this present world to that city yet to come, which we seek (par. 2).

At a time of Christendom's wane, the liturgical reforms of Vatican II were an attempt to reinvigorate the liturgy with the potency of holding together an alternative vision of the world. That purpose was unfortunately subverted by much post-Vatican II liturgical experimentation, which went instead in the direction of embracing and incarnating the visible and secular vision of the broader society. Our liturgical practice demands thoughtful attention if it is to serve as the centerpiece of an incarnate Christian culture. But beyond the proper ordering of the liturgy, an apostolic age demands the weaving of a complete fabric of daily life, of common and personal practices and visible reminders that speak of the invisible world.

5. Rethinking priestly life and education in light of the current cultural context

It was noted previously that families serious about their Catholic faith are finding it increasingly necessary to make adjustments in order to thrive in an apostolic and missionary situation. The same is true, yet more compellingly, for priests. Family life and its rhythms have a certain natural quality that allow at least some sympathy and affinity with almost all human societies. But apart from the understanding of the world that Christ and the Church bring, the priest is an ambiguous figure and his role in life does not make sense. It is thus incumbent upon the Church in a missionary age that she pay special attention to the education of priests and to the shape of their lives, not just morally, but in its overall atmosphere, all the more as the priest has a special responsibility to carry the Christian vision for all the faithful. Our current mode of training priests and the typical shape of priestly life as we now experience it were developed during a Christendom time, and they depend upon a Christendom society for their reasonable functioning. The collapse of Christendom is therefore leading, not surprisingly, to a crisis of priestly life. It is an urgent need of our time to devise ways of preparing priests and of providing avenues of priestly life such that they are ready to meet the new demands of an apostolic time.

In a Christendom age, the priest is a known and understood member of the society. Everywhere he goes his identity and role are recognized. He still has a serious personal task before him, to conform his heart and his behaviour to Christ and to serve those under his care with charity and zeal, but he is not likely to forget who he is and why he has been set apart for service. He was brought up as a child with an implicit understanding of his calling, the whole of his environment reminds him of it, and the overall vision of the society helps him to make sense of his life and his duties. In such a society, a good-hearted priest who is sincere in his calling will probably find his way. His path is fairly clear and well-trodden, and his task will be to perform what is expected of him with faith, diligence and charity. For his preparation, in addition to learning his sacramental duties, he will need to be trained in theology such that he can be a reliable source of Christian truth for those he serves. His formation in character and his overall vision of the world will already be largely in place. The seminary can build upon the wider cultural environment and will be doing its task adequately if it deepens and purifies what is already present in the seminarian from his membership in his family and his society.

The current apostolic environment is different. Those who step forward for priesthood — at least the majority of them — will need not only theological training but also a conversion of mind and vision, coupled with a corresponding transformation of behavior that counters much of what they have imbibed from the wider culture. The patterns of life and ways of thinking that have surrounded them from their childhood, often subtle in their operation, will have to be re-ordered, not just toward a Christian moral code, which may already be in place, but toward a holistic Christian narrative and vision. As such, recent efforts to implement a robust preparatory or spirituality year in priestly formation — a sustained opportunity for personal healing, intellectual conversion, and cultural "detox" — are precisely in line with the needs of our time.

And once ordained to priesthood, there is much in the cultural environment that will tend to the destruction of priestly life unless proper measures have been taken to secure it. In an apostolic age, articulating and building a sound priestly life is necessarily a communal venture. Only under exceptional circumstances would a general attempt to sustain an attack on well-defended enemy territory by sending individual soldiers against it one by one. In an apostolic age, it is equally imprudent for priests to think that they can survive in an enemy-held culture, much less prevail against it effectively, by taking it on singly. Christ himself did not attempt this, but always went about in a company, and the early apostolic missions were made of bands of apostolic workers. In an apostolic age, it is not enough for a priest to be good-hearted and sincere, excellent and necessary as those qualities are. Sending a priest alone and unprepared into the current culture is like sending a soldier alone and without defence against a well-armed fortress. Sincerity alone cannot win this kind of battle.

The question here is not so much whether our current priests are devout or not, hard-working or not, sincere in their calling, or worthy of praise as good servants. It has rather to do with the objective organization of priestly life to a specific end. Does our priestly formation provide the context for the kind of transformation of mind and vision necessary for our apostolic time? Does the typical pattern of priestly life, whether diocesan or religious, tend by its overall shape to give the priest what he will need to accomplish his task well and to live a holy and fruitful life? Does its atmosphere inspire those under its influence with a holistic Christian vision? Here a candid examination would yield the conclusion that neither our current priestly formation nor the present configuration of priestly life is particularly well-ordered to perform these apostolic tasks. A diocesan priest who wishes to incarnate these virtues will often be fighting against, rather than moving with, the grooves of priestly life ahead of him (the same could also be said for at least some religious priests). He will be forced to construct the architecture of his priestly life more or less on his own, and the challenges are many. He can easily become isolated, thereby making his own witness to brotherly love less real. He will operate independently by the necessity of circumstances, needing to find his own way in most of the details of his life. He will find himself affluent, if not outright wealthy (at least living a physically comfortable upper-middle class life, often with access to wealth beyond his own means at the hands of generous members of the faithful). He will find himself more or less alone in planning evangelistic initiatives. He will be very busy such that he will find it difficult to sustain a regular life of prayer and difficult also to maintain habits of study that will keep his mind alert and his preaching fresh. He will be vulnerable to overdoses of entertainment media, which will be a burden to his life of chastity and to his own sense of the sacred and through which he will be imbibing, often unconsciously, the narrative assumptions of a non-Christian world. He will have no obvious mechanism in his life for fraternal correction and, if he begins to stray, he may go a long way down a dangerous road before he is checked. In general, he will struggle to foster an overall Christian vision of life in the midst of a culture that promotes a different vision and a different gospel. This will make it difficult for him to maintain apostolic zeal during the long years and decades of his service, and he may easily fall prey to fatigue, cynicism, laxity, and even despair.

That many priests do not succumb to such temptations and do follow a road of zeal and holiness and enterprising apostolic activity is a testimony to their quiet heroism and to the grace of God. But given the current situation it is not surprising that many priests do not manage to avoid the looming pitfalls. The numbers who leave, who fall into public scandal, or who settle into an unhappy and tepid priestly life witness to the genuine difficulty. Many of these are good-hearted men who might have fared differently had the shape of their lives been more conducive to their apostolic calling. And for those who do manage to live in prayer and charity and apostolic zeal, the energy required of them to sustain such a life against the grain of their surroundings can be exhausting.

Sorting out how best to articulate and live the apostolic priestly calling in the modern post-Christian world will be a task for a whole generation of priests and will no doubt be accomplished in many different ways. In any event, the kind of remedy that is needed is not likely to be found in what is often called "priestly support," which tends to the therapeutic and is satisfied by supplying a modicum of friendship and an occasional opportunity for the priest to talk things through and be understood. Such remedies are likely insufficient to meet the challenges of an apostolic age. It is not so much emotional support that is needed, but rather a whole structure of life within which a priest can exercise his calling for the sake of others. The priest needs to live in and be animated by a Christian vision and a pattern of practices that touch every aspect of life: a pattern ordered to loving obedience to counter the perennial idol of pride; ordered to chastity to counter the aggressive eroticization in the wider culture; ordered to poverty to counter rampant greed and debasing consumerism; ordered to fraternity and common life to counter isolation and fragmentation endemic to modern life and to provide a witness of brotherly love; ordered to prayer, liturgy, and the unseen world to stay in touch with the most important aspects of reality; ordered to austerity to fight the enervating push toward comfort and to maintain missionary zeal; ordered to charity and to effective preaching to reach hearts with the Gospel; ordered to love of the Scriptures and to theological study to be able to catechize and teach the Faith and to meet the intellectual challenges of a highly sophisticated age; and ordered to common initiatives to spearhead a new evangelistic mission. And running through all is a vision ordered to the deep joy of a life given for love of Christ and in imitation of him, configured to him in priesthood, consecrated entirely to him and to his service.

The point of this discussion is not so much to construct a list of desirable priestly virtues; it is rather to inquire into the overall pattern of seminarian formation and priestly life within which a priest actually lives and exercises his role. In the midst of the current post-Christendom context, does that formation and pattern of life tend to the clarity, holiness, and apostolic zeal of the priest who willingly embraces its contours? The current configuration may have worked well enough for many priests in the past. But a pattern of priestly life that was adequate to one cultural setting may be insufficient, and perhaps irresponsible, in another.

6. Allocating resources with apostolicity in mind

In a transitional time such as ours, those entrusted with leadership will need to lend their attention both to the maintenance of the existing institutional order and to the development of apostolic initiatives. Because apostolic works are often not immediately productive and require a different mode of thinking, the tendency can be to starve them of resources and to simply keep "working the system." Under this scenario, when a Christendom way of ordering Church life and institutions proves ever less viable, available resources diminish and are spread ever more thinly until, at a certain point, massive institutional collapse ensues. Instead, without simply abandoning the existing institutional structure, the need is for significant resources to be given to developing the kind of apostolic initiatives that produce conversions, especially among the young. There is probably no easy calculus for determining when a given institution or initiative is worth salvaging and when it needs to be let go or pared down and resources given elsewhere. It is a matter of continual prudential examination of the overall apostolic situation.

Such allocation of resources cannot be done without serious "political will," since it will mean, for example, that parishes may have to share a pastor while other priests are spending their time in what will seem less important or less productive activities. The analogy might be to an army in fallback mode, needing to abandon a certain territory in order to gather strength for the sake of a renewed attack at a later time. They won't give up ground that they can maintain, and they won't give up anything easily; but they will assign some of their soldiers to prepare fallback positions, and when it becomes clear that a certain bit of ground can't reasonably be held, they will perform an orderly retreat. They will invest most of their fighting energy in what is strategically most important. The alternative is to hang on by the fingernails to every acre of ground until the collapse comes and the army is routed, with no possibility of counter-attack.

This principle applies, on a large scale, to a diocese or a school system or a religious order, but it also needs to be applied to each local instantiation of the institution: each family, parish, school, and local chapter of an organization. In an apostolic age such as ours there is no guarantee that things will keep operating merely because someone shows up as the manager. Without genuine conversion of overall vision and serious formation of mind among individual members, the institution will become lost or slowly disappear. Pastors, school administrators, and others in positions of institutional leadership will need to have an eye for the apostolic, keeping a lookout for genuinely committed disciples among their members and finding ways to nurture them. The aim is to create an "apostolic-friendly" environment that will encourage creative missionary initiative.

An apostolic mode of running institutions tends to their renewal, but such renewal in the Church always comes from (relatively) small numbers who are given the grace of an intensity of spiritual life for the sake of the whole body. There can be a natural desire to want to see all boats rise together. For some, this means that whatever initiative is attempted needs to be done by everyone. Any group or organization with a more than usually vibrant life of faith produces uneasiness, and immediately there is an attempt to find some way to "spread the fire around" so that everyone participates. It is of course true that a gift of faith given to an individual or a group is meant to be a treasure for the whole Church, but it becomes so precisely when those who have received it are faithful to the charism they have been given. To try to spread such a gift around indiscriminately is like removing logs from a burning fire and spreading them one by one on the ground in order to distribute the heat better. All that happens is that the fire goes out. Those in roles of responsibility need to understand the dynamism of apostolic renewal in order to promote and nourish it rightly. Not everyone will participate in such renewal in the same way or with the same energy or at the same time.

7. Being ready to put up with a certain apostolic "messiness"

When there is genuine conversion taking place, and especially when it touches the young, there is excitement, a sense of growth, and an immediacy of the power of the Gospel. But it is also true that living, breathing disciples make for more problems. Unenlightened zeal, rigoristic attitudes, idiosyncratic or even heretical stances held with great energy, rivalries between individuals and groups, can and do arise. For the stolid administrator this is nothing but trouble, and after all, dead bodies are much easier to arrange than living ones. But the Church needs to be ready for this kind of energetic messiness if she wants to remain alive and capture the wider culture. Those in leadership positions — bishops, priests, seminary rectors, directors of institutes of various kinds, parents, and teachers — should have an instinct for the apostolic and should welcome apostolic energy even if it means taking certain risks. The Church has a long history of handling such energy and should certainly not be afraid of it. Jesus had a special love for James and John, the "sons of thunder," even if he needed to rebuke them occasionally. And his choice for the apostle to the Gentiles was potentially a very difficult case. One wonders what Ananias and the others whose task it was to help Saint Paul into the local Church at Damascus shortly after his conversion must have felt. He was hardly the model seminarian too often posited by a sleepy and decaying Christendom — friendly, mild, and no trouble. Sometimes it is better to have to tame the over-zealous than to try to convert the skeptical and inspire the apathetic.

8. Expecting cultural influence to be exercised primarily by impressive witness

In a Christendom age, much of the influence of the Church is exercised from the "inside" of the society. Christianity has a privileged place in the culture, its representatives are given a respectful hearing, and much can be accomplished by diplomacy, cultivation of relationship, and maintaining influential positions. The art of the political, understood in a good sense, comes to the fore as a means of guiding the culture toward Christ. The difficult task is then to see that those who gain positions of influence and cultural authority are not themselves corrupted by greed or desire for power or fame. In an apostolic age, influence is exerted less by political arts than by a living witness to the Gospel that captures the imagination. The ancient world, which early held the Christian movement in disdain, was greatly impressed by the courage of the martyrs, by the care Christians gave to the poor and the sick, and by the moral probity of the lives of uneducated believers. These witnesses to the Faith contributed to the eventual conversion of the culture. We are moving again toward such an apostolic age.

In a time such as ours, many will be attempting to exercise influence in a Christendom mode, from the inside, and they will find the returns diminishing and the effect increasingly corrupting. The possibility of influencing the society in this way becomes ever less likely, and those who think they are making headway will often come to find that they have been used by others whose interests are vastly different. A change of attitude is needed. The Church in such a time needs to cultivate a spirit that pursues her true vocation heroically and that spends less time being concerned with what the wider society thinks. This will allow the kind of witness to the Faith that *can* have a profound influence and can ultimately help to convert the culture. The witness of Mother Teresa and her sisters is an example of the kind of daily heroism called for in such an age.

Pope Paul VI's famous assertion that modern man is more willing to listen to witnesses than to teachers, quoted at the beginning of this section, is perhaps best seen in this light. We can tend to interpret this profound insight according to the individualistic and moralistic vision so common among moderns and thus think that he is mainly talking about impressive personal moral action taken by individuals. While his meaning certainly includes such action and points to the need for Christians to live the faith we profess if we hope to gain any kind of hearing for the Gospel, this does not tell the whole story. Such impressive and visible moral actions are not so easy to come by; much — if not most — of Christian moral heroism takes place away from the public eye. Another look at Mother Teresa will signal a yet fuller meaning of what it means to witness to the Faith. Mother Teresa did more than personally care for those on the fringes of life, as beautiful as that was. She went on to establish an order of Sisters whose life and way of being witnessed to a whole vision of the world. By their homes, their prayers, their chastity, their simplicity of life, their cheerfulness, and their labor on behalf of the poor, the Missionaries of Charity have compellingly incarnated and expressed to others a different way of seeing everything. They have made common witness to the great treasure to be found in Christ, to the superfluity of riches, to the love of God for every person no matter how obscure; and for millions around the world, Mother Teresa's blue and white sari has become an icon of the love and mercy of God. In an apostolic age, the Church's most potent and truest witness comes in this fashion, in her communal life, all aspects of which point to the reality of the invisible world.

It is not an uncommon error for those attempting a pastoral and evangelistic strategy in our time of transition to move in exactly the wrong direction as regards Christian witness. Having become accustomed to a situation in which the majority in the society are members of the Church, they have taken majority status as normative for all times, as the only authentic posture for the Church within the society. When many are leaving the Church under the influence of the ruling non-Christian vision or, while still remaining Church members, are complaining about doctrines or disciplines or aspects of its moral vision that don't square easily with prevailing cultural attitudes, some in the Church want to adjust or do away with the "difficult" aspects of the Gospel in order to keep people in the pews. For those with this view, the worst possible situation for the Church is to find that the majority are not with them. It seems a sign that they are failing in their fundamental task, despite Jesus' words about the wide and the narrow way, the many and the few (cf. Mt 7, et al.). Thus, they attempt a kind of compromise in the hope of remaining contemporary and relevant. If the world will not allow itself to be raised to the level of the Church, the Church will have to lower itself to the level of the world. While the motivation for such accommodation is understandable, in practice this way of proceeding proves ineffective (to say nothing of the question of faithfulness to the Gospel). In an apostolic age the Church needs to be not less, but more exacting of her members; the distinct lines of her life and vision need to be made clearer, not mistier. By such a distinctive witness, her true influence upon the society will be exercised.

There is a flip side to this attitude toward Church life and witness. Just as the Church will demand more from her own members in an apostolic time, she will expect less from those who are not her members; she will not demand of those who are not genuinely converted to a Christian way of seeing and of living to abide by the way she orders her life or even to understand how and why she does so. To expect this is to keep thinking in a Christendom mode; it is to insist that everyone in the society is or should be Christian, at least materially. Rather, the Church's primary stance before an unbelieving world is not the imposition of law, which assumes knowledge of its existence and purpose, but the invitation, under an attitude of mercy and hope, into a relationship with the living God and incorporation into the new humanity, to an entirely new way of being and of seeing, one that liberates and that brings meaning and joy.

This double stance toward the Church and the wider society can be difficult for many American Catholics, not only because it signals a new and seriously challenging time (a sobering prospect on its own), but because during the last half-century or so there has been an unconscious embrace by many Catholics of an American narrative vision by which the United States is seen, effectively, as the Church. A strong strain of the American mythical narrative views America as the hope of the world, the true "salt of the earth." Few Catholics would express it this way, but the underlying assumption is present and potent. One can see its influence in the investment of a kind of religious fervor in American patriotism, in the practical attitude that the most important issues we face are sorted out in the realm of politics, and in the loss of fundamental hope when it seems that America is "losing its way." For those who have assumed this vision, a kind of transposition occurs. The legitimate concern that the worldwide Church, called to be a light to the world and inhabited by the Holy Spirit, remain faithful to Christ and be held to a high standard of purity in her mission for the sake of humanity's salvation is repackaged as the concern that America be faithful to its founding ideals lest the world go astray. Whether that American salvific mission is seen as the dissemination of capitalist democracy or the remaking of the world through the U.N.'s millennial goals, the error is the same. Whatever have been the genuine virtues and accomplishments of America, which are surely not insignificant, and however good it would be that America remain faithful to the best of its traditions, such a view of things has little to do with the Christian faith and is miserably inadequate to the genuine need of humanity.

We should be clear about this: even as we love our country and hope that it prospers and exercises good influence beyond its borders, we know that America is in no sense the hope of the world. That honor belongs to Christ alone as he works through his body, the Church. There is nothing surprising, nothing that should touch our Christian hope, however sad and unfortunate it might be, that America would be susceptible to the corruptions of a fallen humanity. The Blessed Mother was immaculately conceived, not the American Republic.

V

The Key Task: Conversion of the Mind to a New Way of Seeing

> In the course of history, this [the Church's apostolic] mission has taken on new forms and employed new strategies according to different places, situations, and historical periods. In our own time, it has been particularly challenged by an abandonment of the Faith — a phenomenon progressively more manifest in societies and cultures which for centuries seemed to be permeated by the Gospel. The social changes we have witnessed in recent decades have a long and complex history, *and they have profoundly altered our way of looking at the world.*
>
> — POPE BENEDICT XVI, Ubicumque et semper

THE MAIN evangelistic task in an apostolic age, a task that also needs to be directed at many within the Church, is the presentation of the Gospel in such a way that the minds of its hearers can be given the opportunity to be transformed, converted from one way of looking at the world to a different way.

In a Christendom age, deeper conversion to Christ usually means taking more seriously the *moral* teaching of the Church. Most of those who live in such a time accept a host of dogmatic and overarching visionary truths: they believe there is a God, a heaven and a hell, a spiritual world of angelic and demonic beings, a judgment to come. They know, at a notional level, that this life is a preparation for another. These truths and this vision may be asleep in them, hardly influencing behavior, but they are still present. In such a context, when a person comes to deeper conversion and determines to pursue the Faith seriously, the result is seen mostly in the moral sphere: a readiness to keep the commandments and to do what is known to be right. In a Christendom time, much of preaching and teaching assumes the whole Christian narrative and centers its attention on emphasizing obedience to the Church's moral precepts. This is natural enough, but it presents problems when the Christendom imaginative canopy is no longer in place. It can give rise to the view, often unconsciously assumed, that to be a Christian means to live a life of moral probity and nothing more. A comment like: "I know atheists who are more Christian than a lot of people at Church" is indicative of this attitude. The whole of the Christian faith tends to be reduced to following a specific moral order.

In an apostolic time, those who present the Gospel, whether to their parishes or to their families, should assume that the majority of their hearers are unconverted or half-converted in mind and imagination and have embraced to some degree the dominant non-Christian vision. The new evangelization aims at the renewal of the mind, because it recognizes that people's minds have been barraged by a daily onslaught of false gospels, leading to confusion and distraction away from invisible realities to concerns solely of this world. Preaching in an apostolic age needs to begin with the appeal to a completely different way of seeing things; it needs to offer a different narrative concerning the great human drama; it needs to aim to put into place the key elements of the integrated Christian vision of the world within which the moral and spiritual disciplines the Church imposes find their place.

It is a strategic mistake to preach solely the moral vision of Christianity before the mind and overall vision have at least begun to be transformed. It is putting the cart before the horse. The reason so much of the Church's moral teaching falls on deaf ears in our time is because it makes no sense according to the ruling vision of the society. As long as that vision holds sway in an individual mind, teaching about moral truth (except where Christian moral precepts line up with those of the ruling vision) will be ineffective and will produce either bewilderment or anger.

To take an example outside the strictly moral realm that still touches on it and elucidates a need of the time: it is often noted that a large percentage of Catholics in America do not believe in the doctrine of the Real Presence. They look at the Eucharist as symbolically and ritually meaningful but not as a transformation of bread and wine into the body and blood of Christ. Some in the Church respond to this situation by saying that we need to be clearer about what the Church teaches; their view is that apparently many people do not know what that teaching is. While there may be simple ignorance of Church teaching in play here, a more significant factor is the lack of a sacramental vision of the world. Living in our culture and embracing its ruling vision, such Catholics have assumed as self-evident a materialistic, "scientific" view. If a thing looks like bread, tastes like bread, has the chemical composition of bread, then it is bread. A priest saying some prayers in the midst of a particular rite doesn't change that. Likely enough, many Catholics who say they believe what the Church teaches about the Eucharist in fact don't quite. They may acknowledge it out of a desire to be obedient, but it has no real meaning for them; they would not know how to go about defending it, and their conviction is fragile and easily lost.

What is necessary here is a conversion of mind to a sacramental vision of the world. Not just at Mass, but all the time, we are living in a sacramental reality: we inhabit both a visible and an invisible world; we make our way through an intermingling of the seen and unseen such that what happens on the visible plane has implications in the vast invisible world. Our bodies are sacramental, a mingling of the spiritual and the material; the Catholic understanding of what and how we eat, what we do sexually, how we treat those who are sick or dead, are pointers toward the way the whole world works. Plunging a person into water really can, under the right circumstances, transfer an immortal soul from the kingdom of darkness to the kingdom of light. We walk in the presence of powerful invisible angelic beings not only when we might happen to think about them, but all the time. Touching another person involves two beings in spiritually meaningful contact. The world is an enchanted and dangerous and momentous place in which we are working out an incomprehensibly high destiny that transcends space and time. This view of the world is consonant with what natural sciences have discovered, but also goes beyond it. Once the realm beyond the natural world is seen and embraced, a whole set of doctrines becomes easier to understand and believe.

What is true of the Eucharist and the sacraments is true of much of Catholic practice in other areas, as well. Catholic teaching on sex makes sense when embedded in a Catholic vision; it makes little sense under the subjectivist naturalist default vision of the current culture and can even appear morally bad. Obligations to attend Mass, duties of faithfulness in a difficult marriage or of obedience to incompetent superiors, the meaning of suffering, the very existence of a saving doctrine that needs to be believed, come alive to the understanding only when they are perceived as the natural outworking of a cosmic reality. This means that the exposition of the Gospel, in preaching and teaching and liturgy and architecture and the arts, needs to accent this conversion of mind. There needs to be a counter-narrative to the overwhelming non-Christian narrative currently on offer. The Christian mythic vision (the true one) needs to be made available such that it can chase out the false myths of the day in the minds of believers and inquirers. Once this happens, questions of morality and Church discipline and articles of faith become easier to sort out. Until it happens, there will be half-conversion at best and a confused and often inadequate response to the Gospel. Such conversion of mind is especially needed in those who lead: in bishops and priests, parents and teachers, writers and scholars and artists. The great apostolic task of our time is to gain a genuine conversion of mind and vision.

If this is true, an obvious question arises: how do the current cultural vision and the Christian vision differ? What are their broad outlines? Adequately to answer that question would demand a far more thorough treatment than can be given here: the confusion of the modern mind makes difficult a neat summary of its sometimes self-contradictory and often fragmentary vision, and no one Christian can claim to have the definitive say on how the Christian vision should be articulated. But it may be of use to note, even if incompletely, some of the more obvious lines along which these mythic narrative understandings go forward. We will consider first the Christian way of seeing, and then we will sketch out the modern, progressive vision.

It should be noted that emphasizing the importance of the overall narrative and imaginative context of the Faith is not meant to suggest that careful theology, clear philosophy, detailed catechesis, and serious moral exertion are somehow unimportant. It is rather to say that all of these essential activities of the Church's life will find their fullest expression and have their greatest effect when they are united in an integral view of the cosmos.

Concerning the Christian Way of Seeing

Christianity is the most shockingly momentous view of what it means to be human that has ever been seriously believed and pursued. The weight of this momentousness is both thrilling and terrifying. Much of the modern flight from Christianity, when it does not stem from boredom with a watered-down conventional version of the Faith, is precisely a flight from the seriousness of existence at the heart of the Christian vision, a refusal to attempt to scale the heights that all humans are called to in Christ.

In the Christian vision, to be a human is to be involved in an extraordinary adventure. The greatest adventure stories ever written are only echoes of it, pale shadows of what the lowliest human is in truth undergoing. This drama began before we were born and will continue after we die, and each of us has been given a unique role to play in it.

An integral aspect of this drama is that we have been born into an invisible world as well as a visible one, and the invisible world is incomparably more real, more lasting, more beautiful, and larger than the visible. Our blindness to that world represents much of our predicament. We are caught by the illusion of the merely seen and need to have our blindness cured. This drama involves us not only with the awful and marvelous and incomprehensible being of God, who created us with a decisive purpose in mind, but also with a cosmic struggle among creatures of spirit more powerful than we are, who influence human life for both good and evil. We have been born into a battle, and we are given the fearful and dignifying burden of choice: we need to take a side.

Every human has been created for a magnificent destiny that makes the greatest prizes of this world seem like uninteresting nothings, a destiny of such height that the imagination can hardly take it in. Not only are we meant to know good things, happiness, strength, length of existence, but we have been created to experience the unthinkable: to share in the very nature of God, to become — in the language so beloved by Eastern Christians — "divinized." Created from the passing stuff of the material world fused with an invisible and immortal soul, we are each of us meant to be what we would be tempted to call gods: creatures of dazzling light and strength, beauty and goodness, sharing in and reflecting the power and beauty of the Infinite God.

Yet our destiny is at great risk. Had it not been for the intervention of God himself in our history by a shocking act of humility and love, our divine destiny would have been lost to us by our own pride and rebellion. Individually and as a race, we had sustained a mortal wound and forfeited our original purpose, becoming enslaved to evil spiritual creatures who themselves had turned their backs on the goodness and light of God and had become deformed and filled with malice.

The true history of the human race has been largely hidden; events of great significance take place away from the eyes of the world. By many orders of magnitude, the most important event in history was the coming of God himself among us in human form. He came not only to teach us truth but also to do battle for us against the powers of darkness, and having conquered them, to revivify us, individually and as a race. He gave his life as an offering to bring us back from the dead and to adopt us into his own divine nature. It was an event hardly noticed by the powerful and wealthy of the time; most knew nothing of it at all, and those who did treated it as of little importance. But that event has since come to echo through every corner of the world. This pattern continually repeats itself: the same hidden momentousness is true in the history of every individual. The real importance of a human life, not only in terms of its ultimate goal but also as regards its influence on current human affairs, is impossible to gauge by anything we can immediately see.

In coming to help and save humanity, God did not just intervene from outside. He conferred on us the high dignity of becoming one of us; he arranged matters such that a human might have the honor of conquering the enemies of humanity. He then established a society in the midst of a darkened world, a kind of colony of heaven that he inhabits and with which he clothes himself, and he gave to all who followed his lead a share in his own life, along with great responsibilities and notable powers to continue the work of saving and healing the human race. The fortunes of that society, and the ongoing story of God bringing humans from slavery to divinity, is the central drama of humanity, compared with which the rise and fall of whole nations and civilizations is of no lasting importance.

The current visible world will come to an end completely; the invisible world, of which each of us is part, will last forever. We are creatures on trial, given the opportunity by God's mercy to work out our salvation, individually and communally, in "fear and trembling" (Phil 2:12). Our great task, the whole of our existence here, is to find and embrace our true destiny and to help others do the same by receiving and embracing the offer of mercy made to us. There are two and only two possible destinations for each human: to gain the life intended for us as members of a renewed humanity and offered to us through the God-made-man, or to turn obstinately from that life and end as immortal failures. For each human, both are real possibilities, and there is no evading the choice: we must seize either the one or the other.

Because we are not yet where we belong, not geographically and not in terms of our final creation, it follows that we cannot be fully happy during this life. We are creatures undergoing a testing of heart, awaiting our true home. When this visible world comes to an end and all is re-created, an event that may occur at any time, there will be a final assessment of the whole human race. All stories will be told truly, all secrets brought to light, all lies melted away. Christ will then determine who has responded to the free gift of forgiveness and so has been found worthy to "enter life," to enjoy the kingdom of light and immortality. For those found worthy, all their piercing longings for perfection, for communion and love, for justice, for fulfillment, for beauty and goodness, will be triumphantly satisfied in a dance of joy and communion, and they will experience what they were created for.

This very brief time that we are given to live on earth is thus at once both immensely significant and of little importance: unimportant in itself and significant in what it prepares us for. Christians hold matters of this world lightly and at the same time take them very seriously. They are not impressed by the scramble for money, fame, power, and pleasure so characteristic of our fallen race, knowing that such things have no ultimate significance. But they realize that in dealing with even the smallest details of life, they are working out an eternal destiny. They fight the darkness within themselves and embrace the life of love laid out for them by Christ, delighting in conforming their wills to his, knowing that obedience to him does not limit them or impede their self-development but rather brings them to their true selves, to freedom and fulfillment. They live as exiles, in hope and hard fighting, waiting for the final triumph of God, full of gratitude for what they have been given, full of hope for all they have been promised, full of love originating in Christ toward others who need to hear the good news of a merciful and forgiving and gift-giving God. They live in the visible world with the invisible always in view; they inhabit time in the constant recognition that they hover at the edge of eternity; they live in lowly disguise while waiting to be clothed with strength and immortality. They rise by falling and ascend the height of divinity by recognizing and repenting of their sins and willingly taking the lowest place with Christ. They fire their minds with the lives of the saints, those champions of faith in whom Christ and the new life he brings have been most influential. They battle for goodness and truth in order to gain a kingdom.

A life like this, characterized by the love of God and of others, lived as a member of the new humanity, no matter how troubled by suffering, no matter how obscure or difficult or filled with seeming failure, is a triumphant success that will end in a crown of blessedness and beauty. A life of great material success and fame and achievement but without love is a dismal failure that will end in darkness and eternal decay.

THERE IS NOTHING in the above inadequate description of the Christian vision that claims any originality; others could no doubt give a better account. What is important for an apostolic age is its narrative and mythic character. Too often Christianity is presented to the mind of the modern believer or inquirer as a set of rules one follows, or as a number of unattached doctrinal statements one accepts, or as an organization one belongs to; but Christianity is not often enough presented as a way of seeing the whole of things. It can even appear that the rules and dogmas get in the way of human happiness. To be apostolic in vision (to repeat an earlier point) is to recognize that Christians don't see *some* things differently than others: they see *everything* differently in the light of the extraordinary drama they have come to understand. To be apostolic is to do more than assent to a set of doctrinal truths or moral precepts, essential as they are; it is to experience daily the adventure that arises from the encounter with Christ; to view events and people moment by moment in the light of that vision; to be caught by the perilous and joy-filled work of learning to be transformed into divine beings headed for eternal rapture in the exhilarating embrace of God.

Concerning the Modern Progressive Way of Seeing

Since the dissolution of the Christendom vision, there is not any one single imaginative vision that has predominated in the Western mind; it is rather a chaos of confusing bits and pieces that do not easily fall together into a coherent whole. It is a blurred and often myopic way of seeing. Nonetheless, there are certain prevalent tropes that have come to undergird most of its variations. The point of naming these elements is not to examine them philosophically or critically; it is rather to identify the assumed first principles that give the vision its mythic potency. Modern progressives (which to some degree means nearly all of us) like to pride ourselves on our rational and scientific way of seeing things. But the power of the modern vision is not in its scientific accuracy. Its most captivating sources come not from reason and science but from romantic utopianism. Modern progressives are, as a group, remarkably impervious to genuine data. We first embrace theoretically conceived utopian ideals and then insist that the evidence fit our mythic visions, whether they be egalitarian, or feminist, or economic, or environmental, or sexual.

1. Faith in progress

The overarching narrative vision that first emerged in the seventeenth and eighteenth centuries in the West both borrowed from and contended against the Christendom vision out of which it arose. Among the most important of those borrowings was the belief that history was "going somewhere." The Jewish view of history, embraced and expanded by Christians, had held that the whole of human history was a story with a beginning and an end: not sound and fury signifying nothing but a dramatic narrative whose author was God. According to that narrative, the human race was progressing not only through time but from lower to higher states: from nothingness to created beings, from fallen and mortally wounded creatures to sons and daughters of God filled with divine life, and ultimately, for those who gained the Kingdom, from flesh and blood to glorified spiritual embodiment and full participation in the divine. The whole of the Christian mind, taught by Christ, was thus oriented to the future. Along with the apostle Paul, Christians were forgetting what lay behind and were pressing on toward the upward call of God (Phil 3:14). At the hands of the Enlighteners, this heavenly vision was taken over and transformed into an earthly vision of perfection in space and time. What for the Christians could ultimately be accomplished only by God in a dramatic culmination that would signal the end of history was now to be accomplished by human effort alone within the confines of historical time. The perfection of the race was still in view; but the means, the conditions, the origin of that perfection had entirely changed. Visions of a humanity in perfect peace and contented prosperity, living by justice and practicing virtue, not in some distant "pie in the sky" world but here and now, danced before their eyes. This is why the modern vision can reasonably be termed "progressive."

This progressive vision was more than just a hope of progress toward good things. It was faith in the ineluctable march of humanity on an ascent to an ever better and happier state of being. Greatly taken by the results of applied science in manipulating certain aspects of human life in a limited sphere and imaginatively captivated by theories of evolution, the modern mind came to believe that not only technologically (which made sense) but also socially and morally (which made no sense), the human race was on a *necessary* upward course. We came to think that we were superior to our ancestors, not just in rapidity of transportation or information flow, but in moral probity and wisdom about non-technological aspects of life — and this by the simple fact of being born later. Every dismissal of a particular moral stance or spiritual practice or time-honored bit of common sense with a phrase like "that's so old fashioned" or "c'mon, it's the twenty-first century" or "let's be on the right side of history" signals the unnoticed assumption of the doctrine of progress. Without such an assumption, such phrases would be fatuously silly. But no one thinks them silly because the assumption of moral progress is so universal; it is one of the first principles of the modern mind.

Bringing the hope of a perfected human society into historical time has a great deal of potency. But it brings also a new relationship to the world. Because the world is seen to be perfectible, and because we are the ones who need to accomplish that perfection, the progressive vision has given rise to a great impatience with imperfection of all kinds. It had long been a moral impetus in Christianity to be concerned for the suffering: to feed the hungry, clothe the naked, care for the sick, ease the burdens of old age. These were all aspects of the command to love one's neighbor. In the Christian vision there had been no question of entirely solving the problems of poverty or sickness or aging outside the sovereign action of God; such conditions were part of the blight of fallen humanity — and only its most visible aspects. Worse than any of them was the state of sin and separation from God that impoverished the whole human race and of which all these physical manifestations were only the outward expression.

One loved and helped those in need not because one was "fixing the world" but because they were God-created beings with a divine destiny, because in a special way they were sacramental representations of the poverty and hunger and sickness of everyone, and because to do so was to participate mystically in the self-forgetful charity of Christ working through his body.

In the modern progressive vision, concern for the poor and the sick has remained, but with a difference — one subtle enough in its first expressions but ultimately bearing serious consequences. Under the influence of a utopian vision of a society perfected by human energy, humble love for the poor was inevitably transposed into proud hatred for poverty; love for the sick became hatred for disease; love for the elderly turned into hatred for the ravages of age. The point was to arrive at a certain this-worldly state of physical and social health. What then was to be done if there were too many poor people to be reasonably enriched, or too many people with sicknesses that had no cure, or too many elderly people who were debilitated by effects of old age that could not be reversed or mitigated? By a perverse but necessary logic, the solution has been to eradicate the poor, eliminate the diseased, and euthanize the aged. According to the modern narrative the point is radically to solve the problems of humanity; suffering is therefore offensive and embarrassing and not to be endured. Pride, rather than love, is the root motivation.

When the broad lines of the progressive vision were first spelled out and preached, hopes were high for a radical transformation of the human race that would occur just around the corner. It was a new dawn, a re-creation of humanity, a break with the whole dark history of the race. There was a touching, if in retrospect remarkably naïve, confidence that evil could be overcome, justice established, vice conquered, and the human race brought to peace and goodness simply through the efforts of energetic people with the right ideas and the knowledge and skill to implement them. But the gospel of progress has not delivered on its promises, except in the one area of increasing human technological power and thereby of providing greater wealth and physical comfort. After the horrors of the twentieth century, to conclude that the human race is inevitably becoming morally better is to shut one's eyes to mountains of evidence. The same lesson has been taught by the implementation of many plans and programs for social and moral betterment. The massive failure of the Soviet communist attempt to build a perfect society is only the most glaring example of failure across the board. Even when genuine good has been accomplished, it has fallen so far short of what was promised that the progressive gospel has become difficult wholeheartedly to believe by any except the young, who don't yet have contrary experience and can be taken, for a time, by the heady wine of a Woodstock-like experience. These unfulfilled promises have left many of us in a precarious position. We often still speak the language of the progressive vision in politics and economics and social planning and academics; it is the only one on offer. But how many who are working in government or social services or the academy or business can believe the rhetoric? This explains the prevalence of a common type among us: the well-intentioned but disheartened and slightly cynical progressive. No longer quite believing that the world is undergoing a necessary transformation toward goodness, yet retaining a sentimental attachment to a lost youthful ideal and still wanting to do something positive along the way, the typical modern progressive has ceased dreaming great dreams and is mostly concerned to construct a meaningful and comfortable personal life, while still doing what might be possible to make at least some kind of difference in the world.

2. Denial of the Fall

An essential contour in the modern progressive vision is the denial of the Fall as part of the explanation for human evil. Christians had long taught that the human race was caught in a curse of its own making and that one of the key sources of the world's evil was the wound in each of our hearts caused by pride and rejection of God. G. K. Chesterton once famously responded to a London newspaper's request for essays on the question, "What's wrong with the world?" with a two-word reply: "I am." Chesterton meant that for the Christian, the first and most important task in making the world a better place is to be attentive to one's own conversion. The progressive vision, by contrast, while aware of evil in the world, finds the source of that evil elsewhere: it is not the result of an internal wound in each human, but the bad fruit of ignorance, whether of physical laws or social structures or psychological principles. There is no need to engage in the humiliating and continuing battle to forge a new heart within; evil could be undone and goodness established by gaining and applying the requisite knowledge.

Having discounted the evil in each human heart and having little time for the idea of personal evil in fallen angelic beings, the progressive vision still needed to identify a source for the prevalence of active evil in the world. That source has always been found in a particular group of people who have been deemed to stand athwart the march of human progress. It might be the aristocracy, or the Jews, or the bourgeoisie, or the Catholics, or the homophobes, or the breeders, or the reactionaries, or the whoever. Over against them were the pure, the enlightened ones, those "on the right side of history." Having relegated demons to the nursery, every utopian progressive vision finds itself constrained to demonize some portion of fellow humans. This has led to great injustice and at times to some of the most barbaric treatment of humans in history; but it is not seen that way by those under the influence of the progressive myth. According to the Christian vision it was the devil alone who was to be opposed with a perfect hatred; fellow humans were to be treated with respect, and even enemies, shockingly, with love. That at least was the ideal. Under the progressive vision, it became proper to hate certain other humans with the perfect hatred once reserved for the devil. Such an attitude, expressing itself in events like the Reign of Terror, the Gulag, the Holocaust and the abortion mills, has been justified by the concern to bring about the promise of perfection granted by the progressive vision. Thus, the denial of the Fall inevitably brings with it a culture of death, not because its proponents set out to kill, but because the utopian ideal runs up against a fatally flawed humanity. The only options are either to eradicate those whose perceived weakness or evil keep the dream of the new humanity from being realized or to give up the project altogether.

3. Marginalization of God

In its manifold forms, the modern narrative myth is constant in this: it marginalizes God as an actor in human history. Sometimes this is expressed in an explicitly atheistic narrative, but often it is not. Most commonly, the modern vision does not say "God does not exist," but rather, "God does not matter," which comes, practically speaking, to the same thing. Under the modern progressive vision, one can reasonably attempt to make sense of one's life, sort out one's friends, pursue one's love affairs, decide on questions of marriage and family, arrange a career, order the affairs of government, establish and maintain justice, handle geopolitical relations, determine what is right and wrong, all without recourse to the divine, without consulting the creator of all who "upholds the universe by his word of power" (Heb 1:3). The modern vision involves what might be called practical atheism, whatever the personal belief of many of its possessors might be.

Hence, under the modern progressive vision, religion is instinctively held to be so very private a matter. Americans like to be religious, but we also like to customize our religions to our personal preferences. We are not interested in religion as an account of reality; it is rather something that enhances our experience and helps us deal with the stress of existence. We are not so much seeking a Lord as looking for a therapist. "Whatever works for you" is a reasonable dictum under such an understanding. Should a given religion become a source of friction because its adherents claim it to be an account of universal truth, it provokes immediate hostility. It is no surprise that a historically irresponsible statement like "religions have been the greatest cause of wars in history" can be taken seriously by modern progressives. Its acceptability is not due to its accuracy but to the way it conforms to and supports the progressive myth.

There is an unfortunate by-product that comes from marginalizing God: one wakes to find the universe a boring place. God is the one supremely interesting personality, and a world that banishes him also banishes its only genuine source of animation and interest. This explains something of the massive boredom of the modern age. Because we have no engrossing and abiding interest that engages the whole of our minds and personalities, we need to be constantly titillated and distracted. When seen as reflections of the infinite creativity of God swept up in a momentous drama, all things, even the least significant, hold interest. When God is absent, nothing — not art nor politics nor sports nor sex nor the pursuit of money nor even "the most interesting man in the world" — can keep boredom and disillusion at bay for long.

4. Intoxication with the world of space and time

It is almost a definition of Christian conversion to call it the process by which a person comes alive to the invisible world in all its ramifications. "We look not to the things that are seen," says Saint Paul, "but to the things that are unseen. For the things that are seen are transient, but the things that are unseen are eternal" (2 Cor 4:18). This is a restatement of Jesus' teaching about laying up treasure in heaven where there is no rust, and no thieves, and no moths (cf. Mt 6). The unseen but real — God, angelic beings, human souls, the heavenly throne room — holds first place in the Christian vision as being of primary importance. Things that are seen take on importance only as they reveal and open up the unseen world that interpenetrates and upholds them. This is the meaning of sacramentality. The modern progressive vision is almost the antithesis of sacramentality. Under the modern vision, we look constantly, eagerly, incessantly, with anxiety and hope and longing to the things that are seen. Whether we hold, theoretically, that there are unseen things as well hardly matters. We are distracted and delighted and dismayed by the things of time and sense, and we attempt to make our lives meaningful according to their logic alone.

In the modern progressive vision, it becomes natural to consider human relations and the entire structure of daily life in political terms. We think that world peace and social contentment can be achieved if only we erect the proper political structures and set up the right programs. When a problem arises we look for a political solution; we attempt to handle complex human matters by establishing policies and protocols; we live by publicity and polls; we think we are in touch with "the way things are" if we watch a lot of news programs.

Under this vision it is natural that we spend so many billions of dollars on health care and that doctors and psychologists reign as high priests of the culture. It is natural that we think economic prosperity the beginning and end of human success and consider those who are not prosperous as marginalized and oppressed. It is natural that we are offended by suffering and do everything in our power to maximize our comfort, even to the point of insisting on a comfortable death. It is natural that we think the most important questions facing us have to do with the planet and its viability. It is natural that we are obsessed with physical appearance and the luxurious trappings of success. It is natural that we carefully calculate whether and how many and what type of children we would like to have according to an equation of immediate enjoyment and often determine to have no children at all or do away with the ones we have 'accidentally' conceived, since they are prohibitively expensive and a great deal of trouble. It is natural that we hold to a narrative of success limited by the date of our birth and the date of our death, one that carries with it pictures of interesting friends, fulfilling careers, dynamic and meaningful sexual relationships, fun and adventurous experiences, and a golden old age.

Noteworthy in the progressive vision is the loss of the momentous: the disappearance of a final judgment, the lack of a sense that humans are undergoing a sifting and a testing that will have hugely practical consequences beyond this life. The progressive vision allows for no hell, and while most still think of or hope for a heaven, they do so in a vague and misty way. The only meaningful criteria for judging success or failure are those that can be seen: popularity, power, wealth, comfort, and personal enrichment.

And because we are actually immortal souls created to dance with the living God, called to an eternal destiny that won't stop haunting us, it is natural under such a vision of smallness that we fall into creeping despair and attempt to medicate our misery by taking huge doses of the true opiate of the masses — electronic entertainment.

5. Freedom to choose as the essence of human dignity and the source of human happiness

In the modern progressive vision, "freedom" is an incantatory idea. The modern narrative is a story of liberation from oppressive forces. To maximize human freedom is seen as a self-evident moral task and a self-evident source of human happiness and human dignity. Despite the complexity of what the word 'freedom' might mean, what it has and hasn't meant at different times, what are the many and often hard-to-establish conditions for its promotion, how many difficult questions there are to be unraveled in a simple phrase such as "humans are meant for freedom," nonetheless in the progressive lexicon freedom is an unproblematic word denoting a simple idea. Let any cause, any program, any activity, any person, be claimed to promote freedom, and it is assumed that we are dealing with a simple good. Let something be thought to get in the way of freedom, and it is clear that it must be swept away. Much of the mythic power of the progressive vision comes from its claim to champion freedom and, by that means, to provide ever-increasing dignity to humans.

Freedom is a concept and an ideal that has been at the heart of western civilization from its origin among the Greeks and its penetration by Christianity. The whole of the Christian hope has been summed up by saying that, in Christ, the human is set free: from death, from devilish tyranny, from destructive passions, from ignorance, brought to the status of sons and daughters of God as free men and women. To be a free human was the highest goal of the civilization; the traditional education in the liberal arts was geared to help achieve this aim. Involved in this classical and Christian understanding of freedom was the idea that we were most free when we became most fully what we were meant to be, when we approximated most truly our given nature. To become free under the Christian mythic vision was therefore to grow into a particular image, one given us by the God who had created us and according to which we would find happiness and goodness. Freedom was thus not an arbitrary concept, but rather a task with a goal. The accomplishment of freedom always demanded serious discipline according to what was good and true and right.

In the progressive vision, freedom has come to mean something different: the possibility of choosing whatever my individual will desires at whatever time. I am most free when there is nothing impeding me from doing what I wish to do, and I will be most happy and most fully human and dignified when I am most free to choose my own will. What is right and wrong and how I conceive my own existence is my own choice. To be autonomous (a law unto oneself) is the greatest good. The most dignified person is the one who has self-identified, who has determined who and what he or she (interchangeably) will or will not be.

Such a view inevitably, if unwittingly, makes God into the great enemy of humanity. If there is a moral and spiritual order that originates outside of myself, if there is an intention in my creation and a nature given to me, then I am not absolutely free to be my own creator, and my autonomy is at risk. To protect this autonomy, God is always put at the margins of the modern myth. If he exists at all, he is a vague and misty principle that allows for almost infinite malleability, a kind of miasma of spirituality that will allow me to construct my own sense of self and of the world around me.

The insistence on autonomy in the progressive vision has induced an intoxication with breaking things that are thought to stand in the way of personal freedom. Freedom is to be accomplished not in the careful construction over time of the conditions under which humans could have the opportunity to achieve their true nature, but rather in the bursting of bonds that hold the individual will in check. Under this vision, revolution gains a kind of moral magic as the privileged instrument of freedom, and the tearing down of Bastilles, whether they come in the form of moral norms or social conventions or religious traditions or oppressive governments, is the self-evident task of serious people. This explains something of the strange barbarity of so much of modernity. Despite its sophistication, its gilded rhetoric and high hopes for good things, it has a destructive core. It promises a social and personal paradise, but saddled with a false understanding of humanity and its ills and thinking that the desired utopia will arrive as a matter of course once the requisite restraints have been demolished, it too often leaves behind not a lush garden but a howling wasteland.

6. Consumer contentment the default experience

For all the grand utopian elements in the progressive vision, for all its impressive narrative power, in practice it provides little for the individual person to live by from day to day. After all, we each inhabit a universe of our own, and we need to have aspirations and ideals for our personal world. High sounding phrases like "making the world a better place" and "helping the future of humanity" and "fighting for hope and change" are too vague in meaning and too loose in accomplishment to sustain us. We need a narrative closer to home; we need to know that each of us is walking a daily path leading to personal fulfillment, and here the progressive utopian vision provides little to nourish us. As a result, the default vision that many live under is one of consumer contentment. We exercise freedom by buying what we want; we find meaning by keeping abreast of the "next big thing"; we make the world a better place by carefully constructing a personal statement of existence whose brand is produced out of the consumer choices we make. Ironically, the stirring proclamation of the progressive gospel to remake and perfect the human race by banishing God and seizing our personal destiny in our own hands winds up for most of us in online buying or in a shopping mall. “We have nothing to lose but our chains!” has devolved into “Shop till you drop!”

Conclusion: Readiness to Embrace the Times We are Given

> Let us go forward in hope! A new millennium is opening before the Church like a vast ocean upon which we shall venture, relying on the help of Christ. The Son of God, who became incarnate two thousand years ago out of love for humanity, is at work even today: we need discerning eyes to see this and, above all, a generous heart to become the instruments of his work.
>
> — POPE ST. JOHN PAUL II, *Novo Millenio Ineunte*, 58

THE MODERN progressive vision is all around us, incessantly hammered home with all the pervasive power of electronic imagery and consumer affluence, but compared to the one given us by God, it is a weak and anemic vision. From its beginnings its claims have been unreal, and it has been so weakened by generations of dismal human experience that it can now be sustained only by economic prosperity and the apparent lack of a good alternative. The hope that mankind would be made better has in practice been replaced by the hope that we can build yet faster and more powerful phones and screens; the dreams of a perfected world of justice and freedom are ebbing into vague hopes of biotechnological enhancement of physical powers. Much of the current strength of the modern vision is in its immediacy: it appeals with great skill to the human propensity to be distracted by the sensual and the seen. But it offers little of substance to the deepest aspects of the human person: it is intellectually bankrupt and spiritually impoverished. It should not therefore be a source of intimidation or anxiety for Christians, who have a much more compelling way to understand the world and a much richer life to experience and to offer our fellow pilgrims in this world. It is not coincidental that so much of the entertainment eagerly pursued by the young minds among us involves epic dramas, cosmic battles among powerful spiritual forces for good and evil that demand of the young hero or heroine extraordinary character, commitment and sacrifice for the saving of the world. What the progressive vision tossed out the door has snuck back, in mutilated form, through the window. This should not surprise us: those who have been deprived of the real thing will grope after pale substitutes.

The Holy Spirit is at work in every age, ours included. If it is true, as we are assured by Saint Paul, that grace is more present the more that evil abounds (cf. Rom 5), we might expect an especially abundant action of the Holy Spirit in our own time. Our task is to understand the age we have been given, to trace out how the Holy Spirit is working in it, and to seize the adventure of cooperating with him. May we be given the wisdom and the courage to rise to the challenge of the new apostolic age that is coming upon us and to prove faithful stewards in our generation of the saving message and liberating life given us by Jesus Christ.

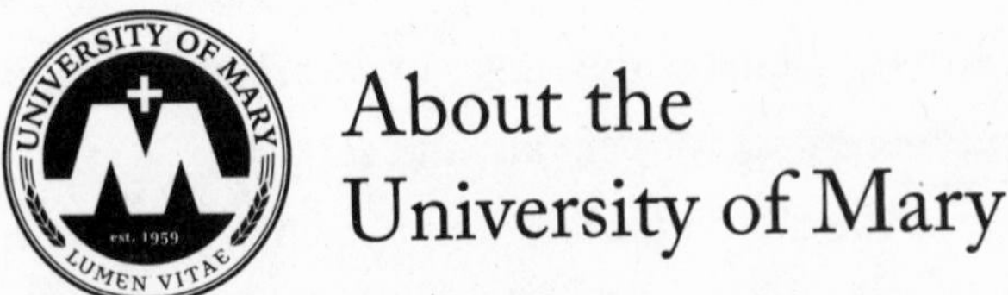

About the University of Mary

The UNIVERSITY of MARY is a private, co-educational Catholic university that welcomes students of all faiths and backgrounds. The university has its origins in the St. Alexius College of Nursing, opened by Benedictine Sisters in 1915. In 1947, these Sisters established Annunciation Priory in Bismarck, a monastic community independent of the original motherhouse in St. Joseph, Minnesota. Meanwhile, the nursing college evolved into a two-year women's junior college, and in 1959, the Sisters founded Mary College as a four-year, degree-granting institution. Full university status was achieved in 1986. The University of Mary has been accredited by the Higher Learning Commission of the North Central Association of Colleges and Schools since 1968, and continues under the sponsorship of the Benedictine Sisters of Annunciation Monastery.

Since its beginning, the University of Mary has sought to respond to the needs of people in this region and beyond. Enrollment grew quickly from 69 students to more than 3,800 students today. The university offers more than 50 undergraduate majors, 15 master's degree programs and four doctoral degrees. Classes are conducted at the main campus and other facilities in Bismarck; online; at satellite locations in Arizona, Montana, Kansas and North Dakota; and at a campus in Rome, Italy.

The University of Mary educates the whole student for a full life, characterized by moral courage and leadership in chosen professions and service to the community. Every aspect of academic and social life is infused with the Benedictine values of community, hospitality, moderation, prayer, respect for persons, and service.

Already one of the most affordable, high-quality private universities in the nation, the University of Mary now offers 'Year-Round Campus,' a unique college-career option that enables students to earn a bachelor's degree in just 2.6 years and a master's degree in four years. This greatly reduces costs and allows students to begin their careers much sooner. The University of Mary offers exceptional educational value, as well as outstanding scholarship and financial aid opportunities. Within six months of graduation, 95 percent of graduates are working or pursuing additional education.

Scholar athletes at the University of Mary participate in 18 varsity sports in NCAA Division II.